Train Spotters

A personal countdown to the end of steam on BR in 1968

By

Mike Priestley

Title page and back cover images from the sixties with thanks to Ian Hughes.
All the other photographs were taken by the author unless otherwise stated.

First Published 2010 by Countyvise Limited,
14 Appin Road, Birkenhead, Wirral CH41 9HH

British Library Cataloguing in Publication Data.
A catalogue record for this book is available from the British Library.

ISBN 978 1 906823 54 2

Foreword

I was just in time for the end of steam on BR. More accurately, I was privileged to be around as a teenager to witness the last few years of activity, leading up to its official demise from the national network in 1968.

I grew up on Merseyside during the heyday of the Beatles, but only one out of our close knit group of friends got to see them live and that was because his mum was trying to set him up with a young lady. We were just fourteen in May 1963, so what was she thinking of? She bought Andy two tickets for the Empire Theatre in Liverpool and he could hardly say no. Not that the rest of us have held a grudge for nearly half a century, or anything….

It was an exciting time for music and we were in the thick of it but our other interest frequently took centre stage at the same time. Hindsight is an amazing concept. With it, I would surely have made more of an effort to go to places on the rail network I never reached in time. I would have loved to have experienced some of the pinnacles of railway folklore, like full trips on the Waverley and the Somerset and Dorset routes, but I left it too late.

It just did not look that bad when we got together as a group of mates in1960. We naively assumed things would pretty much carry on as they were. As the decade wore on we wised up a bit and in the end there was a strong realisation that we were witnessing changes of significant proportions. It was too late by then and by 1968 the future for railway enthusiasts looked bleak. There followed a complete ban on main line steam, in the interest of portraying a clean, modern image for the national network of the future.

Christian Wolmar commented on the period that became so pivotal to us in his excellent book, Fire and Steam, "…..the railway industry clung on to steam technology for far too long and the train spotters had a field day as British Railways continued to build locomotives right up to 1960"[p.268]. Well, thank God for that.

This book contains pictures taken with a succession of less expensive cameras. I owned then retired, sold for next to nothing, part exchanged or binned an Ensign [our family camera throughout the 50s], Kodak Brownie 127, Coloursnap 3, Halina Rolls, Kodak Retinette 1A, and a Practika. The truth is that it is too easy to blame the cameras. I never realised I was making a visual record of an important period of time. I just hoped I was getting a reasonable image of a steam engine to show to my friends.

Retrospectively, I could have been more thoughtful about composition, the light issue and timing. Results suggest I could also have tried harder to keep the camera steady more regularly.

I became intoxicated with train spotting, denying myself the pleasure of other aspects of the hobby early on in the quest for "cops", meaning engines I had not seen before. It was the collector in me. I don't know if initially it was the residual hunter gatherer gene manifesting itself, simple escapism from the pressures of adolescence, or if it was meeting some deeper psychological need. The process of making collections certainly became very important and it has stuck with me in one way or another, ever since.

In addition to the essential attraction of the steam engine and its eventual longevity, Christian Wolmar goes on to point out that train spotting itself is a peculiarly British phenomenon and a post war one at that. He highlights Ian Allan's influence in that respect, as he was the first to list the locomotives and publish them in pocket sized books.

That allowed us to make sense of all the numbers and to impose order on the whole business and consequently, they were essential purchases. Most large stations had a W.H. Smith kiosk or stall which stocked them. So did a very conveniently located newsagent's shop on the opposite side of the main road and a stone's throw from the frontage of Crewe station. We had to pass it on the walk to Crewe North sheds, so it was visited frequently.

The consensus amongst the commentators seems to be that the continued use of steam traction for two decades after the war was a costly mistake, at a time when many other railway systems worldwide were developing more economical diesel and electric options.

The decisions to carry on building to established pre-war steam locomotive designs and even to initiate a range of new ones suited us fine, though it was probably not the most sensible decision for the railways, especially considering the very short eventual life span of a lot of the Standard classes that were subsequently developed. While British Railways lost opportunities to modernise the service, as spotters, we benefited from a period of inertia.

Lack of cash, though, inevitably meant that much of our spotting was done close to home and arguably we were a bit out on a limb, compared to kids who grew up in Doncaster or Tamworth. We went train spotting by bike, to Bidston shed with its North Eastern connections with the former GCR exemplified by its complement of J94 tanks and to Birkenhead MPD and its array of heavy freight engines.

We even extended our spotting activities to ships. We often took our bikes to Liverpool via Seacombe Ferry on Saturday mornings and cycled the length of the dock system from Gladstone back to the Pier Head, sometimes including a selection of the now closed South Docks as well. We noted the names of the ships of the various merchant shipping lines, including Clan, Blue Funnel, Harrison, Brocklebank and many more. Sometimes we took in both trains and ships on the same outing, taking a route through the Birkenhead dock system via the Penny Bridge, Duke Street Bridge and the Four Bridges on our way to Mollington Street depot in Birkenhead.

We were invited on board a Clan Line boat in Liverpool Docks by a group of foreign seamen and climbed a narrow and rather flimsy set of steps up the ship's side to reach the deck for a look round. The resulting and fairly brief interaction with our hosts relied entirely on gestures and facial expression, primarily that universal common characteristic, the smile.

The narrow wharf side between the walls of the transit sheds and the edge of the dock was strewn with all sorts of bits and bobs; grain, pieces of timber and a range of spillages, as well as being interlaced with railway lines that were sometimes very wet and slippery. It was an accident waiting to happen. Below us lurked the cold and dirty water of the dock itself and vertical dock walls. I couldn't swim in those days, either. Yet we were never stopped at the dock gates, nor apprehended en route by any one in officialdom. We survived.

We bought spotting pocket books for ships as well, which were organised in similar fashion to the Ian Allan locomotive books and we underlined them as we saw them, just like the trains. Towards the end of the week, I would go into Earlston Library in Wallasey and peruse the columns of the Liverpool Journal of Commerce, to see which ships were coming into specifically named docks, by the following weekend. Yes, we were properly hooked on spotting things. By the end of the decade two of us were even going to evening bird watching classes led by a local vicar at the nearby technical college. That hobby has stood the test of time as well.

Obsessive collecting during this period was not confined to engine numbers, ship names and eventually, to bird species. Whilst still at junior school, I remember standing on street corners near home in order to list vehicle registration numbers. HF plates were registered in Wallasey, whilst CM and BG traffic was from Birkenhead.

While my younger sister took advantage of parental encouragement towards self improvement, by learning to swim with George at Guinea Gap Baths and by embarking on piano lessons in an elderly spinster's front room in Vyner Road, instead, I set about filling my bedroom with stuff.

At one time or another after that I obtained armies of minute plastic soldiers, piles of comics [Beano and Beezer, then Victor and Hotspur], Brooke Bond tea cards [of birds, which you could swap at a local general store], match boxes, book matches, cigarette packets, postage stamps, Airfix kits [planes and trains], bubble gum cards, fireworks [seasonal, much to my mother's relief], autographs, pin badges from youth hostels, sew-on cloth badges from the different parts of the country I had visited, records [singles, EPs and long players] and beer mats.

I had also subscribed to and then amassed large quantities of the various railway magazines during my teens, including at different times, Trains Illustrated, Modern Railways, Railway Magazine and Railway World. I eventually forfeited some of my copies of Trains Illustrated in order to make a frieze out of photographs of steam engines, which I had cut out and attached to a roll of wallpaper and placed most of the way round my bedroom wall.

The remainder blocked up wardrobe space for years, probably vacating my childhood family home about the same time as I did. I'm pretty sure my girlfriend and I had come to an amicable agreement by then about their future, which would have involved them starting a new life together elsewhere.

Chapter 1
Before 1962

What is it about railways? You either like them or you don't. Not sure? Why not take the level crossing test?

This is how it works. You are in the car and as you approach the level crossing the lights flash, the barriers come down and you draw up to the car in front and turn the engine off.

Do you think?
[a] Blast, I'm going to be late.
[b] Great, I wonder what's coming.

As long as I can remember I have been a [b].

I have tried to unravel it backwards to my infancy. I believe I had an advantage in that I suspect that my dad was a closet train man. He never really said so, but he did put trains in my way rather more than might have been expected from someone without any interest at all.

Dad never collected numbers but he certainly fostered my involvement. He bought me some colour coded regional railway time tables and even the infamous Beeching Report, without any direct prompting from me. I found its contents interesting rather than alarming.

The first visible piece of evidence that railways might be important for me in the future was taken in my grandmother's garden in Winchester, in the summer of 1954. I had at my disposal my cousin's Hornby "O" gauge, clockwork train set.

I was not very interested in branch line Britain then. There were not many engines in those quiet country back waters. I was going to be quite obsessed with main lines, however. That was where the action was. Initially, it was my dad that took me there.

He later told me that as a toddler, I was taken to the park next to the line out of Manchester Piccadilly in Alderley Edge, which was close to my grandmother's house. Here, I would apparently climb the steps of the slide and watch such delights as the Pines Express, The Mancunian and The Comet go by. To say this memory is hazy is an understatement. So too, is the occasion Dad took me on the Liverpool Overhead Railway in 1953, to see the burnt out hulk of the Empress of Canada in Liverpool Docks.

My own earliest clear memory of seeing a steam train is walking down the platform at London Waterloo to view the unrebuilt Bulleid Pacific, which had brought us up to the capital from Winchester in 1953 or 1954. From that moment on it was not just the railway that was of interest, but more specifically, the steam engine.

So much has already been written about steam locomotives and why people find them so mesmerising. I only want to add that for me it was a sensory and aesthetic thing from the outset, rather than a mechanical one. I still, to this day, could not adequately describe in detail exactly how they work, nor indeed could I name most of their bits, once you get past the obvious ones, like wheels and pistons.

At the end of the day after junior school in Wallasey, my mum would sometimes allow a detour on our way home to our cul-de-sac in Liscard so that I could cast a glance at the Seacombe branch, which ran through a cutting near the bottom of the school yard near Liscard and Poulton station. We went to the bridge in Mill Lane to look down the steps onto the station site. Trains on this line were few and far between, but I well remember the occasional plumes of smoke that were visible from the school playground.

Our first family home was very much in the centre of Wallasey, which was then in the County of Cheshire. When the wind was in the south east there was often a nasty smell in the air, which was popularly attributed to the soap factory at Port Sunlight, but I suppose it could sometimes have come further, from the chemical works at Ellesmere Port. This was before the passing of clean air legislation and at a time when everyone burned coal domestically.

Periodically and especially on foggy days and in winter, of course, when air pressure was high and there was little wind to move things on, this smoke got trapped at ground level as smog. The fog horns wailed mournfully and repetitively on the Mersey. Under those circumstances it was literally not safe to go out and bronchitis was a common ailment.

The first car in our road, CHF 600, a Ford Consul, was owned by a junior school teacher. I was invited to go to his house to see my first cup final, on his small and hazy black and white TV screen. This was the game in which Bert Trautmann played on having broken his neck. He turned out to be a brave German, which did not actually fit in with what we were expected to think of them in the decade after the war, a view perpetuated much longer than that, by popular cartoon comic books.

We knew everyone else in the street of terraced and semi-detached houses and there was a good community feel to the place. There were two elderly spinsters who lived opposite to us and Mum used to take me and my sister round to thank them for our regular birthday and Christmas presents. This was always an old silver sixpence wrapped up in a cellophane sweet wrapper. Both ladies were known to us as Miss Leicester. They only ever wore black and the older one combated her deafness by using a trumpet, which she held up to her better ear, allowing her to just about receive incoming conversation.

By complete coincidence, close friends of ours now own this house and rent it out to tenants. When they were busy redecorating between occupants recently, I accepted their invitation to have a look round. I stood in the light and airy lounge and tried to imagine the scene 55 years earlier, with the elderly ladies surrounded by the dark and elaborate clutter of a largely Victorian drawing room, with heavy furniture, potted plants and sombre colours. It remained a world away.

We were allowed to play outside, but not to leave our road. One winter I built a massive snowman against the lamp post at the end of the street. As soon as it was completed Cain's coalmen, the delivery men who carried the sacks of coal from their lorry down the entry next to each house to reach the coal shed in the back yard, kicked it down in passing. I had just been introduced to injustice.

Looking back, I guess I could have tried empathy. I would never have fancied a job lugging heavy, dirty, sacks full of coal around all the time, even less on freezing winter days. Taking it out on a snowman could be considered a socially acceptable way of relieving the stress. Instead, I chose to maintain a long-standing vendetta that even extended to boycotting beer of the same name for several decades.

Come to think of it, if the coalman hadn't seen to it, the lamplighter, with his bike and his long pole with a hook on the end, would have done it by tea time. That could not have been one of the greatest of jobs in winter, either.

Something of a contrast to our neighbourhood was provided by Aunty Ruth. My mother's sister lived in a lovely house called The Old Rectory, at Cranoe, Leicestershire. We took idyllic summer holidays there, in 1955, 1957 and 1958 and always in August. Wood pigeons cooed in a large cedar tree and peahens strutted their stuff on the patio outside the French windows. From the house there was a wonderful view across a wide vale, of farms interspersed with pockets of woodland.

I made the mistake of going back there more recently. I suppose it was in a nostalgic attempt to recapture the past. The word prairie came to mind, followed closely by pylon. In the 50s you could just make out the smoke from trains maybe two miles away, threading their way through the landscape, on the far side of the valley.

My uncle, a barrister in Leicester, took time off to take us into Market Harborough in his car, a novelty in itself, with strong smells of petrol in the garage and wood polish and leather in the vehicle itself. From next to a river in the park, I have a clear recollection of seeing what I have since decided must have been a Class B1, or something similar and behind it an Eastern Region coach, because it had an oval shaped window near the door.

When my grandmother was suddenly taken ill during our last holiday there, we had to see our mum off in Leicester, so that she could go to administer care in Winchester. On that day, I distinctly registered green carriages in my mind for the first time, though there must actually have been loads of them around on my first journey to London, some years before. Up until then I thought they were all either maroon or blood and custard, like the models I had.

We had distant relations who ran Weir Farm in Cold Hatton, Shropshire. In 1955 and 1959 we stayed with them, travelling by train to Wellington and then on to the house by taxi. During our second visit I marched my mum and dad, alternately and a number of times, to Ellerdine Halt. This was the nearest bit of railway to the farm, on the Wellington to Market Drayton line and there I made them wait for hours to watch trains which never came. I only remember seeing one, but that, of course, made it all worthwhile. I hope my folks agreed.

The first day of our summer holiday away from home was the best day in the year, far outshining my birthday and Christmas Day. Excitement ran at fever pitch. I was given the job of burying the eggshells from breakfast in the garden. I think the reason was something to do with not leaving perishable rubbish in the bin for a long time.

We did not have a car and on that special day we travelled in a taxi to the station, sometimes to New Brighton, but more frequently through the Birkenhead road tunnel under the River Mersey to Liverpool Central for Leicestershire, Liverpool Exchange for the Lake District, or just across the docks to Birkenhead Woodside for Shropshire. It was the only day in the year we went anywhere by taxi. I was desperate to sit in the front.

On the way to Leicester all the trains were steam hauled, as usual. At Manchester Central we had lunch in the cafeteria, while somebody played the piano. It was another world to me. Then we crossed the Peak District on the former Midland Railway main line to Derby, through Chinley and Miller's Dale.

It was from Exchange that we began holidays to Derwentwater in 1960 and again in 1962. On the first occasion, we were met at the station by a resplendent Clan Class No.72000 Clan Buchanan, at the head of the Glasgow express, which would presumably have taken us as far as Penrith, having been united with carriages from Manchester at Preston.

At Penrith our train to Keswick was headed by an Ivatt Class 2 and amazingly, after the first stop, probably at Blencow, the driver beckoned me forward to the engine. He had noticed me, I guess, with my head permanently on a stalk, out of the first carriage window. This remains one of the railway highlights of my life, a quite spontaneous and unexpected cab ride as far as Threlkeld.

The driver explained that for me to arrive at Keswick on the footplate might gain him some unwanted attention from his superiors, but I'd had my fix and so I returned delirious to the rest of the family in standard class.

The most memorable thing about the ride was how rough it was, but whether that was caused by an out of condition engine, poor track maintenance or if it was just par for the course, I still don't know. It bucked sideways quite alarmingly and I loved every minute of it. The rest of the holiday was tame by comparison. Even climbing Scafell Pike came a distant second.

I was indebted to my parents for all these opportunities. I know I was lucky. We were not a wealthy family, but we were comfortable enough to be able to take one annual holiday, usually of a fortnight's extent, even though we stayed most frequently with relations. Most families could not afford to get away from home with any regularity at that time.

For a short time my best friend at junior school was John. I went with him to watch my first proper football match. We saw Liverpool lose to Aston Villa from the cage that was the boys' pen at Anfield, Peter McParland scoring the winner for the visitors. The Smiths lived close to us and I spent a lot of time round there, partly because they had a "telly". Although the radio sitcom Life with the Lyons, held no interest for me, life with the Smiths could be quite entertaining.

John's dad worked for the Post Office, in a supervisory capacity important enough for him to gain access for us to Lime Street station signal box, which overlooked the track layout at the tunnel mouth. I also possibly owe him my life. He rescued us both from a sandbank at Harrison Drive, when the tide came up the channel and cut us off. He tucked us under each arm and waded back to the beach

Their house was always a fog of cigarette smoke. Mrs Smith, a very up front lady with a lot of warmth and some dynamism, played hymns on the piano and she pressed me to sing along, having decided that I had a fine treble voice. I preferred to watch Grandstand and the Lone Ranger, but I guess I had to kind of earn it. Then she suggested the church choir. I declined. I'm sure I could have found another friend with a TV if I had needed to.

I don't ever remember being invited to stay for tea, but I noticed in passing through with some frequency that John's sister never ate her crusts. Instead, she threw them over her shoulder and into the open fire directly behind her seat without a glance. She was remarkably accurate. It was quite a skill.

A series of other shortlived primary school friendships followed, as I practised the art of establishing common ground with potential soul mates. Around the time that swotting for my first serious exams should have been at the forefront of my consciousness, instead, I sank briefly into criminal activity. Another boy and I agreed to steal coins from our respective mother's purses, but when his mum noticed a shortfall she blamed me. Confronted by an irate parent, having to splutter denials and at the same time knowing I was as guilty as sin in my own house put me off that game long before my conscience got to work on it.

My mother received £8 a week housekeeping money, transferred from Dad's salary. It was a figure that went unchanged for a long time, presumably before inflation had been invented. She must have noticed the loss of a full half a crown at a time [two shillings and six pence, now 12.5 p]. It was even a big coin, but she never said a word. Even if she hadn't noticed she would have wondered about my sudden lack of appetite as I gorged myself on illicit sweets. She just waited for my shame to kick in, followed by the remorse that lasted for years.

My accomplice and I settled for going to cubs together instead. We would certainly have benefited from the strong moral component expounded there. We wore red neckerchiefs held on with a woggle. There was a lot of standing in line to attention and shouting "dib, dib, dib" and then "dob, dob, dob" and when the time came to move up to the sea scouts I copped out. There was no point me staying on because I couldn't swim, as had already been glaringly ascertained.

Before I left junior school, I remember announcing breezily to my class of forty five and to our teacher that I had been adopted as a baby. I discovered from the response, or rather from the complete lack of any response, that this was still one of a number of conversational taboo subjects in the first year of the swinging sixties.

The comfortable upbringing I eventually received had been touch and go in the first place. My folks had been invited to view a number of infants up for adoption during the post war baby boom. Mum told me later that I clinched it by smiling a lot.

I soon found out that Pepe and his brother were the only other adopted kids in our neighbourhood, or even the whole town, or maybe the world, for all I knew. I was consistently grateful thereafter to my parents for their openness and honesty in telling me the story as soon as they thought I was old enough to understand it. It just meant I had one more thing to be thankful to them for.

Meanwhile Dad continued to play his part in encouraging my interest in trains. On one occasion, we were sniffing around the barriers at Liverpool Central High Level watching the station pilots removing stock from the platforms. I was invited up to make my second cab ride. This time it was on an ex LMS tank, which took me up through the tunnels to Brunswick and back again, no doubt much to Dad's relief, as he waited on the concourse for me to reappear.

If I had been born five years later I would have missed these opportunities to enjoy steam traction as the norm on the national railway system. I started train spotting soon after I began secondary school in 1960. It proved to be an excellent reason for passing the eleven plus exams.

What an abomination they were. To issue life chances at such a ridiculously young age, to separate brothers and sisters, split up friendship groups and to do unimaginable damage to the self-esteem of a majority of each year group beggars belief. I believe they still sit it in some parts of the country, though, overall, the blatantly bi-partite system of my youth has disappeared and patterns of secondary schooling have become more muddied in recent times.

I suspect that specialist schools and academies and a range of other initiatives serve to obfuscate. They baffle the unwary and bypass those with no realistic alternative to their community school and they effectively maintain an advantage for more discriminating parents and those who can afford to move catchment area.

Would it just not be more sensible to spend a few more bob on resources for the comprehensive schools perceived to be performing poorly in order to help them improve? In my experience, the teachers therein are a generally fine and heroic breed. They just need more support instead of the blame they sometimes receive from politicians and the press.

Oblivious of how many of my peers in the last year of the juniors were feeling at being labelled as failures, I was dead chuffed to pass it at the time, political awareness being a year or two down the line yet. The one member of our group to fail actually only became a close friend a couple of years later, by which time his parents had done what was quite common in our relatively middle class enclave and sent him to private school instead, to rescue him from the ignominy of having to attend the local secondary modern.

However, I was delighted, along with all of my carefully groomed class, which was already streamed by ability at the age of nine, to be an official success. I ended up praising to the skies the teacher I had been petrified of for the previous two years. She was a sort of prototype iron lady, stern and dominating, with only the briefest flicker of a wry smile to occasionally indicate that there was another more human side to her. I got to know Jane Turner a lot better after leaving her class. Her son Mark became a good friend and a train spotting companion.

I was invited round soon afterwards to the games room in their attic to listen to his new Roy Orbison record, "Only the Lonely", where I simultaneously received my first ever wasp sting. The formerly very scary, battle axe teacher administered sympathy and first aid. What a turn round. I'd had the cane three times whilst at junior school, admittedly never from Mrs Turner, but it was still like being in the company of another person for the first time, such was the fear that she had previously instilled in me.

Come to think of it my fourth and final primary school had provided quite a strange range of experiences. For example, I distinctly remember having to sit, at one stage, within the classroom in the order of success in what was no doubt a very important internal test, in which I had come 19th out of 45. I shared the two-seater desk with another boy, who presumably achieved 20th position on that occasion. Or perhaps it was the other way round. I reminded him of this recently and he pretended he had forgotten all about it.

I was caned three times across the palm for talking during the school assembly, allotted another three for trespassing unknowingly into the adjacent senior school section of the unmarked playground and three more on a further occasion for a similarly heinous crime, which I have obliterated from my consciousness, so dire was it. I was not, however, punished for weeing a considerable distance up the wall, above the trough, in the uncovered outdoor boys' toilet, at the bottom of the yard. I reached a height that would take some beating and probably remains a record to this day. I assume they were knocked down many years ago, as these days even children are allowed to go to the toilet indoors.

On a purely selfish level the transfer at eleven turned out to be a majorly critical event, because at that time Wallasey Grammar School had a railway society, which I and my friends, old and new, were quick to join. I bet the secondary modern did not even have a railway club, never mind a society.

Better still, this group went on trips to railway sheds and works, in addition to putting on film shows after lessons, in a blacked out geography class room. There, we saw whatever the society was able to get hold of, mainly, I think, British Transport Commission advertising and promotional films.

Instead of relying on Dad to put trains in my way in a rather intermittent fashion, mainly at holiday times, the railway world suddenly got a whole lot bigger for me and a lot more accessible. For this, we were indebted to Jack Dugdale, a maths teacher, who presided over the group, mostly from the relatively safe distance of the school printing press, for which he was also responsible, that was located in a nearby first floor room in the Withens Lane building.

Dad already knew Jack from their time together at Liverpool University. As well as all his other attributes, Jack Dugdale was a railway modeller, who hand built large scale steam locomotives.

Jack had two willing assistants. They were known to us as Abbott and Dyer. It was always surnames at the grammar school. Though they sounded like a comedy duo, they took their roles very seriously. They were senior boys in the school, perhaps three or more years ahead of us, but when we were in the "fags" [so called, because as first year pupils, we were expected to run errands for prefects and other men in school uniforms] they appeared to be all but grown up already.

We gave them a bit of a run around at times. After all, they were fair game because they were not teachers, but they were kind of in charge of us, in this after school get together. I believe that these guys pretty much set the agenda deciding where we went on our trips and taking responsibility for the logistics of each operation, for example, by obtaining shed and works permits. We certainly owed them regular thanks, but I doubt if we ever showed them the gratitude they deserved.

When Jack could not accompany us, we had to press gang another unsuspecting member of staff instead, so that we could claim to be responsibly led by an adult. Most of them only did it once [I wonder why?], but we always found someone when we needed to.

So it was that we went in a large and lively group to Crewe, Derby, Birmingham and York, armed with passes for the various railway installations, always travelling by train and starting our journeys at either Liverpool Central or Lime Street or from Birkenhead Woodside. One of these earlier trips was to Oswestry, via the Class 1400 hauled push and pull service from Gobowen, where the locomotive works was still open and host to one of the distinctive ex GWR Dukedog Class 4-4-0s, No.9014.

In between these trips, from the upstairs physics lab at school it was possible to follow the smoke trails of traffic in and out of Liverpool Exchange station. The tracks ran parallel to, but were raised above, the line of the North Docks waterfront on the other side of the river. Though they were over a mile away, I could concentrate on them far better than the subject I was supposed to be attending to.

If my interest had needed any further kick start, it received it in September 1961, when my new school friend Andy recounted stories from his family holiday to Glenfarg in Scotland about A4 Class No. 60031 Golden Plover and other such majestic creatures, which I had heard about but never seen. Competition over numbers probably began on that day.

As school became the focal point of our organised spotting ventures, then Dad became less critically important as a means to an end, though he always showed interest in the accounts of our visits. Selfishly, I never checked to see if he felt left out after that, but he always came into his own again during later family holidays, well into the mid 60s and at one or two pivotal moments in between.

Civic Society Visit Railway

Mr. A. E. Carridge, chief technician at Edge Hill signal box, explains the workings of an electronic relay device which automatically controls points and signals to eight-years-old Stephen Elliott, of 6 Woolacombe Road, Liverpool.

Stephen was a member of a party organised by Merseyside Civic Society who visited the new Edge Hill signal box and Allerton diesel electric depot, Liverpool, on Saturday.

The party were shown the new electronic control panel at Edge Hill—one of the most up to date in the country—which automatically controls the points and signals along twenty-four miles of route.

It is manned by fifty-five-year-old Mr George Douthy, of 21 Edgar Road, Liverpool, who has been a signalman for thirty-five years. He was given no lessons in the use of the new equipment. "I just picked it up," he said. But he prefers the new-style signalling to the old lever method. "You could come to work in your Sunday suit and not get dirty," he says.

The new signal box has replaced four old-style boxes, and the electronic equipment has almost eliminated the factor of human error.

At Allerton, the party were shown some of the electric diesels which will eventually be used on the Lime Street to Euston route when the electrification is completed.

The trains have 3,300 horse power and are capable of a maximum speed of 100 m.p.h.

Below, Mr. G. Priestley and his son Michael, aged 13, of 19 Elm Park Road, Wallasey, test one of the new electric diesels at Allerton.

This Merseyside Civic Society visit to Edge Hill signal box and the new electric depot at Allerton was reported in The *Liverpool Daily Post* and *Echo*. In the cab of one of the new blue electrics with my dad, I had an opportunity to show off my bobble hat and anorak, which, along with a duffle bag, were surely all the rage and certainly de rigueur for thirteen year old train spotters at the time. I am grateful to the *Liverpool Daily Post* and *Echo* for permission to reproduce this article.

Chapter 2
1962

We grew up in New Brighton, in the County Borough of Wallasey, on the Wirral Peninsula. My family had moved to New Brighton when I was eight years old and it was amazing what a difference a couple of miles made to our quality of life. It was a comfortable place to be and a relatively safe distance, in most respects it seemed, from the murkier parts of industrial Merseyside, now even further south and east.

Our new house was a four bedroom, pebble-dashed semi, built early in the twentieth century. I was very conscious that this represented a distinctly upwardly mobile move for our family. The rooms were bigger and still had the bell pushes in situ, which would have been used to summon the live in housemaid, who would originally have occupied the small fourth bedroom, which we called the box room.

To start with we retained coal fires, at least in the lounge and kitchen, but now they were burning the new, processed and supposedly smokeless fuel. Eventually electric fires and storage radiators took over. The old, black, bakelite telephone would eventually be replaced by a trendy, lightweight, grey plastic version, though still initially with a ring dial. Our phone number was New Brighton 2857, which was also an ex GWR 2800 Class 2-8-0, one which I did get to see at some stage on BR. It now resides at the Severn Valley Railway, one of the many engines rescued from the Barry scrap yards.

Hall Class No. 4921 Eaton Hall on a parcels train at Crewe, taken from the base of the footbridge which led to Crewe North sheds. In my experience Western Region locomotives were not common in the station, though they could be found hiding in Gresty Lane sheds, in the shadow of the Mornflake Oats factory, which was a bit of a haul by foot on a hot day. This undated shot probably comes from early 1962. It is one of four photos that are not tied to specific dates, before my more refined recording system really took off.

In the back garden, in the shadow of a flowering cherry tree, there was an air raid shelter dating from the Second World War. Originally covered in a stone rockery, which my parents had removed, it was a solid concrete structure, the bottom half of which was sunk into the garden. There were steps down to a single small room, where a narrow, rusty ventilation tube was its only other feature.

I christened it the "gozzy ghost cave", for no good reason, other than I was eight years old and it seemed like a good idea at the time. So that everyone knew that I painted it onto the roof in large red letters. I bet Mum and Dad were pleased. I excitedly tried to think of games I could play in it and failed. It was damp, musty and stank of urine, or at least, if it hadn't done so to start with, it soon did. I abandoned it and eventually, as soon as my folks could afford to have it dismantled, it disappeared.

We lived in Elm Park Road, so called, not surprisingly, because it was lined throughout with mature elm trees. Unfortunately, Dutch Elm Disease eventually put paid to them. The local authority resisted any temptation to rename it Narrow Grass Verge Road or Spindly New Sapling Avenue.

We had a fifteen minute walk from our house to the Irish Sea coast in Liverpool Bay to the north and we were five minutes further away, walking eastwards, from the banks of the River Mersey. The river side of the peninsula stank when the tide was out, thanks to the dumping of sewage, presumably partially treated, through outflow pipes, which then ended up on the beach when the tide went out.

Facing north at Crewe station in early 1962 is Princess Royal Class No. 46208 Princess Helena Victoria. There were a lot of school caps and uniforms around amongst the train spotters. This probably reflected the fact that a lot of visits to Crewe Works and elsewhere, at the time, were organised by kindly teachers, following a lot of verbal pressure and attempted bribes from pupils.

Floating stools were known as Mersey goldfish and the state of the water eventually put paid to the annual policemen's swim between Seacombe and New Brighton. Around the corner, on the north Wirral coast, people readily swam in the sea at Harrison Drive, on the few days in the year that were warm enough. Perhaps the discharge pipes went out further there.

The resort of New Brighton was in gradual decline but there were plenty of advantages to our location, including fresh sea air from the prevailing westerly winds and direct rail access to Liverpool from our local station, ten minutes walk from home.

Much of Wallasey, including New Brighton, was semi-detached, suburban housing that provided homes for white collar commuters to Liverpool. Most of the dads we knew fell into this category, getting to work by bus and boat to the shipping, insurance and other offices in the city's central business district, behind Liverpool Pier Head. Our own town's attractions were mainly coastal in nature.

This shot of Royal Scot Class No. 46120 Royal Inniskilling Fusilier was taken in early 1962. On the back of the print, I've written somewhat tentatively, "Chester?" Scots and rebuilt Patriots were easily recognisable at a distance by their curved smoke deflectors.

The lovely Victorian flower gardens at Vale Park tumbled down to the Mersey at Egremont Promenade. At the corner of the peninsula and overlooking the mouth of the river, was the resort itself. New Brighton was still entertaining holiday makers for a week's stay, arriving by special summer Saturday trains from the Midlands and the industrial north west of England, throughout the 1950s and even into the early sixties, though I don't remember seeing any of them arrive.

The outdoor fairground was popular in summer with all the expected rides and stalls in the shadow of the Tower Ballroom, formerly the substantial red brick base for a tower that was higher than Blackpool's in its day. There was Tommy Mann's miniature railway, too, with steam locomotives named "Crompton" and "Tim Bobbin". Added to these, a proper fort dating from the Napoleonic Wars, two lighthouses [including the defunct one at Leasowe], two lidos, one of them the largest open-air swimming pool in Europe and itself an art deco masterpiece, later destroyed in a piece of municipal cultural vandalism, as well as a matching 1930s indoor fairground, now a listed building.

Many of our train spotting trips started nearby, on the third rail electric trains, which linked us to Birkenhead and Liverpool. We always thought of them as being particularly mundane, but I collected all the motor coach and carriage numbers all the same. I believe that New Brighton station had running in boards but no totems, unlike the two other Wallasey stations, Grove Road and Village. The underground, as we called it, was our springboard to the delights of the national rail network.

Some youngsters occasionally took enormous risks by daring each other to cross the electrified third rail. We never got involved. I've always found some of the day to day challenges of ordinary life scary enough, without putting my continued existence at risk for some kind of misplaced kudos. We treated the railway with respect from the outset.

I had found the adjustment to the demands of secondary school quite difficult. I was a little lacking in self-confidence and I feigned illness a few times in my first two years there. I had become an early recruit to the ranks of the worried well. I did get lots of tummy aches, however and I had lost my appetite for long stretches whilst at primary school, culminating in regular visits to the clinic in Merton Road, Liscard.

Here, a collection of pallid and light-weight boys sat around in circle, bare-chested and in goggles, to receive "heat-ray treatment" from a blue lamp, set above the centre of the room. It must have worked, though I was still slight of stature by the time I had moved up to secondary school. By then, my illnesses were increasingly fictitious.

It gradually dawned on me how fortunate I was. There were two deaths in our immediate neighbourhood from childhood leukaemia. Drawn curtains, throughout, was the standard signal to the world of such a bereavement. It was puzzling and scary that people of our age could die so young, in the days before survival rates for this affliction and for so much else began to gradually climb.

Instead, I made the most of my coughs and colds. Either my mum believed my tales, gave me the benefit of the doubt, or else she just recognised that I was uncomfortable and granted me time out, hoping I would eventually find some more resolve.

She was an intelligent and perceptive lady, so I veer retrospectively towards the latter interpretation. I read comics, railway magazines and books instead. I also started planning train spotting trips, a role I kept up over the coming years and expanded when we began to stay away from home for a few days at a time, as guests of the Youth Hostels' Association.

The absence episode was costly to me in that I was demoted within the streaming system that operated in the grammar school at the end of my first year there. It was to be some time before any academic potential was to be recognised in me at all after that, least of all by me. I fell into lethargy over school work, which seemed to be about right, if not actually expected, from the "C" class. There were, however, some characters in there that I found very amusing and my attendance rate gradually picked up as I felt more comfortable being entertained in their company.

The first entry in the train spotting notebooks that I have kept all this time, says that on an undisclosed date, probably in early 1962, I went to Crewe for my eleventh visit there. I had been a train spotter for at least two years by then. Crewe was a big draw for obvious reasons, a busy station, the West Coast Main Line, a large scale junction, 3 sheds [plus a separate diesel and electric depot, which had been added later] and a locomotive works.

The diesels and electrics were already well established by the time we started showing interest, of course, but there was also lots of steam around. There is no indication of where exactly I went while I was there, on this first recorded event, but we certainly toured the works, where Type 4 Western diesels were already under construction in the sequence Nos. D1035 to D1045, inclusive. Peak Class diesels were also being built there and we saw Nos. D54 to D57, in various stages of completion. In contrast and at the end of their working lives were two ex Lancashire and Yorkshire Railway Aspinall Class 0F saddle tanks, Nos. 52312 and 52441.

We saw a lot of engines that day, including nine Coronation Class Pacifics, which we always referred to as "Semis". With the Princess Class Pacifics, they were the stars of the show, right at the top of our hierarchy of desirable engines. Half of the original "Prinnies", as we called them, had been withdrawn by the summer of 1962 and we saw none on that day. I had seen all of them, quite early on in my spotting career, except, of course, for the unfortunate and long time scrapped No. 46202 Princess Anne.

Prinnies were big but not the prettiest for me; long body, short tender, although they did look powerful. I loved some of the names, like Princess Helena Victoria, Princess Arthur of Connaught and Princess Margaret Rose. They were just the right sort of names for engines, especially as engines were supposed to be female. I never associated them with particular members of the royal family. I had no idea who some of those people were and like my folks, I was lukewarm about the whole royalty thing anyway. They were just great names, big important looking curved pieces of metal above the driving wheel. I can quite understand why they continue to command such high prices at railwayana auctions around the country today.

Named Royal Scot Class engines, just referred to as "Scots" and Jubilee Class, called "Jubs" by us [rhyming with tubs], were plentiful, along with a couple of Britannia Class Pacifics ["Brits"]. I also liked the unrebuilt versions of the Patriot Class. They looked old fashioned but quite stately, with their big fat front ends.

Royal Scot Class No. 46139 The Welsh Regiment pulls into Crewe from the north in early 1962. From memory, the track being taken here would have meant the Scot was likely to be on its way straight through the station on one of the central roads, without stopping. Troop trains used to come into that category, surprisingly frequently.

They were a relatively common sight when I started spotting and it could well have been No. 45501 St Dunstan's which hauled us back across the Peak District from Derby, on an early school railway society trip to the sheds and works there in 1960 or 1961. I have no written record of an event I can picture quite clearly in my mind's eye, as she steadily drew her Manchester Central bound train under our platform lights at the end of a chilly visit to the former Midland Railway stronghold.

There were two ways to get to Crewe from home. We either went to Liverpool Lime Street on the underground or we started at Woodside station in Birkenhead and changed at Chester. This was my preferred route. To get to Woodside involved taking a train from New Brighton station to Birkenhead Hamilton Square or an early morning No.10 bus from Stroud's Corner, in Wallasey.

Some of these buses belonged to Birkenhead Corporation and they were blue and not to be confused with the Wallasey buses that shared the cross-docks duties, which were described officially as "sea green", and which were actually and emphatically yellow.

Later on friends Dave and Grah both worked on the buses for a time as conductor and driver respectively. Dave says he believes he knows how the misunderstanding came about. The story goes that an enquiry was made as to what colour the vehicles were to be painted and the reply was to "see Green", meaning to ask Mr Green, who was in charge at the time.

The No.10 was invariably full of workers going to the Cammell Lairds' shipbuilder's yard. It was all flat cloth caps and snap tins, which I think we were more likely to call butty boxes. Upstairs the air was thick with cigarette smoke, but you were lucky to get a seat at all.

Woodside station had an overall roof and it was a dark and cavernous place. The concourse had large uneven flagstones, which seemed to collect puddles of murky water, in spite of its supposed canopy. The platforms seemed rather short and the rails disappeared from the terminus sharply on a curve into a deep, vertical cutting and then, more or less immediately, into a tunnel beneath the town. It was an atmospheric, hemmed in location, where the sound of the steam engines moving off resounded off the surrounding high walls.

The latter part of the line from Woodside into Chester after Hooton station was a bit of a race track and quite a few drivers enjoyed putting the Stanier Class 2 tanks through their paces. Chester was pretty busy at that time and we spent whole days there, even cycling from home occasionally, before settling down for a few hours on the stone steps leading to the bridge taking Hoole Road over the railway at the north west end of the station. Then it was a twenty mile ride back along the New Chester Road in time for tea.

Chester was interesting for its LM/GW mix. As well as all the big London Midland engines, you could see Castle, County, Grange, Manor and Hall Class locomotives, though the totals of each were relatively small. The line to Shrewsbury, and eventually to London Paddington, dealt with through trains from Birkenhead, which reversed at Chester.

On our first listed trip there, we cabbed [were granted permission to join the driver and fireman on the footplate for a short time] Castle Class No. 5023 Brecon Castle. We saw two other Castles that day, Nos. 7018 Drysllwyn Castle and 5022 Wigmore Castle. County Class No.1025 County of Radnor put in an appearance, as did Coronation Class Pacific No. 46228 Duchess of Rutland.

Chester was the venue for the spitting competition. Looking back, this was not my finest hour. Fellow train spotter Pete and I sat on a seat at the far north end of the main down platform and counted the times we could get our spittle to clear the platform edge and disappear onto the track. Needless to say, by the end of the match the platform itself was pretty much littered. The only saving grace I can claim in my defence, apart from my youth, was that few travellers ventured that far down the platform, whilst it was game on.

Amusing yourself during quiet spells and most stations had them, was always a challenge and we only resorted to "yokking" [spitting] on that one occasion. Sandwiches brought from home rarely lasted past about 11.30 in the morning, so we did a lot of roaming around the station, visiting the cafeteria as often as funds would permit.

We would pick our own England cricket and football teams and we would argue over the merits of the tunes of the moment, or list our top ten favourite groups [the term "bands" was still reserved for dance bands rather than rock ensembles at that time]. Much of the rest of the time was spent in conversation about girls or Everton FC. I had a brief flirtation with Leicester City, because of our earlier holiday links, but I was soon persuaded by peer group pressure that Everton might be a more sensible option.

I was helped in this decision by brothers Dave and John, who were my friends and neighbours and more specifically by their dad, who drove us all to Birmingham, Leicester and often to Goodison Park, "The Golden Ground", where I became an instant admirer of Jimmy Gabriel, Fred Pickering and the much revered Alex Young, "The Golden Vision". There was obviously a lot of golden stuff around in those days.

Royal Scot Class No. 46162 Queen's Westminster Rifleman pauses next to the water tower at Penrith, northbound on 21/7/62. This was the first day of our family holiday to the Lake District. Our connecting train service onwards to Keswick this year was in the form of a two car diesel multiple unit. Two years before, on the same route, I had been privileged to enjoy a ride in the cab of an Ivatt Class 2. 21/7/62 was the first date I recorded in my surviving spotting notebooks, though I had been collecting numbers since about 1960.

Back on the station platforms we mimicked the comedians of the day and sang pop songs out loud. Dave was well known for making up his own lyrics, while we tried to stick to the original versions, though, strangely, some of his contrived interpretations often seemed to fit the music quite well. We also talked a fair bit about trains.

We were generally well behaved. We never took journeys we had not paid for. We did as we were told if reprimanded, for example when rocking on the Post Office trailer we were sitting

on, too vigorously. We did not answer people back, preferring to mutter and moan about them when they had moved on. We were not big on graffiti, though I'm sure we must have inscribed station benches with certain girls' names, from time to time.
"I digress", as Ronnie Corbett used to say, or was it Frankie Howard?

Shrewsbury was also easily reachable for the day, via Chester and Wrexham and it was our destination for another trip early in 1962. Much of our spotting by this time was done as a small group of lads on Saturdays, with local shed visits being made on Sundays. These augmented the organised school visits we were also involved in, which were usually planned for school holiday weekdays.

We knew that although most King Class engines on the Paddington expresses came off at Birmingham or more likely at Wolverhampton, it was possible to see them sporadically at Shrewsbury and we were rewarded on that day by the presence of No. 6010 King Charles I. Six Castle Class engines were noted and two Royal Scots, Nos. 46155 The Lancer and 46125 3rd Carabinier.

My Dad sitting in the cab of A2 Class No. 60537 Batchelor's Button, on Carlisle Canal sheds on 23/7/62. Dad had agreed to accompany me to Carlisle and he was very useful in lending the occasion a certain grown up dignity, when it came to asking shed staff if we could have a look round. Alongside is A3 Class No. 60043 Brown Jack. A1 Class No. 60151 Midlothian was also on shed. These engines were magical strangers to me at that time.

On our next trip to Crewe, we saw Standard Class 8P No. 71000 Duke of Gloucester and the experimental diesel No. DP2, as well as two of the Princess Class engines, Nos. 46203 Princess Margaret Rose and 46209 Princess Beatrice. The first in the sequence of the Coronation Class Pacifics, No. 46220 Coronation, was one of eight that we noted on the same day.

I had a model train set which featured another of the Prinnies, No. 46201 Princess Elizabeth in black livery. My Triang layout never gained permanent status, however and although a number of additions were made to the basic package, I think I felt I had to choose between the expense of a commitment to modelling and the cost of visiting the real thing. I chose reality and sold the lot to a pawn broker in Liscard for £5.00, much of which I probably ate as sweets, as my mouth full of metal fillings reminds me.

A springtime trip to Chester in 1962 turned up three Castle Class locomotives, Nos. 5022 Wigmore Castle again, 7025 Sudeley Castle and 7015 Carn Brea Castle. Coronation Class Pacific No. 46225 Duchess of Gloucester also put in an appearance on one of the London Euston to Holyhead trains, possibly the Emerald Isle Express, which, I have a feeling, was sometimes hauled by a Scot.

The walk from Canal to Kingmoor, assisted no doubt by my Aidan Fuller's Shed Directory, took us beneath [or across ?] and then alongside the main line to Glasgow out of Citadel station. At this point we were dwarfed by Coronation Class No. 46244 King George VI as it stormed north towards Beattock and Glasgow. Not for the last time, I got my timing wrong as I pressed the shutter [23/7/62].

There was time for one more visit to Crewe before the summer holidays. I can see from my notes where we must have walked to Gresty Lane sheds, with seven ex GWR engines listed together, including five Halls and a Grange Class No.6851 Hurst Grange. The blue electrics were already in charge of a lot of trains from Euston to Crewe, with steam and some English Electric Type 4 diesels, taking the trains further north.

It was at Crewe that one of us recognised a Coronation Street actor, whose name I can't remember, sitting in a green 4 car electric multiple unit in one of the bay platforms. He was waiting, not surprisingly under the circumstances, for the departure of the train to Manchester. We boarded the train and asked him for his autograph. He seemed less than pleased at being recognised. He told us to work hard at school and "Don't go in for acting.

At Kingmoor shed, even Dad's jacket, shirt and tie and his eloquent middle class voice couldn't swing it with the foreman, so he stood impassively by and enjoyed a Senior Service cigarette, whilst I took a chance in the more accessible areas of the shed, darting around, like some sort of demented flying insect. We made it safely back to Citadel station in time to see Britannia Class No. 70054 Dornoch Firth preparing to leave for the south, presumably over the Settle and Carlisle line, as it was shedded at 55A Leeds Holbeck at the time [23/7/62].

Be scientists or something useful." Feeling rather bemused, we hopped off before we were inadvertently whisked away for a fun journey to Manchester in his company.

The penultimate Saturday in July was again the big day for me, being the start of our annual family holiday. It certainly was the case in 1962, with an early start from Liverpool Exchange. Our journey via Preston turned up a few Jubs and Scots but at Penrith, waiting for our two car diesel multiple unit to Keswick, we saw Coronation Class No. 46231 Duchess of Atholl pass through, with the Caledonian named train.

Keswick station, since closed, was and actually still is in part, quite splendid, as befits an important gateway to the English Lake District. Canopied but spacious and light, with green paint work and big flagstones under foot, it certainly did it for me. Adjoining and still extant, the impressive hotel, constructed in Lakeland stone, welcomed well heeled visitors straight off the trains.

Our accommodation was a little more modest, but it was cosy and very well situated. From the square opposite the Moot Hall in the centre of the town, we took the Borrowdale bus, itself a period piece at that time, reminiscent of the one featured in the Scottish Highlands in the 1950s version of The Thirty Nine Steps. Just before Grange in Borrowdale was reached, we alighted and walked up the lane to Troutdale Bungalow, with its view of Derwentwater and Skiddaw.

The platform for the Oswestry branch at Gobowen on 28/9/62 is occupied by Class 14XX No. 1458 and a single auto coach train. The lady in a tweed suit hurries past the engine driver ready in his cab. The platform trolley provides a reminder of the countless happy hours spent sitting around, wishing we still had something left to eat during the afternoon quiet spell. [How come it was quiet everywhere you went on the railway system, at the same time just after dinner?]

I was almost certainly thinking on our arrival, nice location, but a bit of a haul to get back on the trains. I gave it a day, in the interest of family unity then made my pitch for a trip to Carlisle. On the Monday, Mum acquiesced, Dad went with the flow and we were away. I don't think he ever needed much arm twisting.

No evidence of multiple unit numbers in my notes, so it looks like we got back to Penrith behind Ivatt Class 2 No. 46455. This was one of those unforgettable days, for me. We walked to Carlisle Canal sheds [we always talked about "the sheds" in the plural] and then on to Kingmoor and finally back to the station. By that time we were either too tired, or we had run out of time for a crack at Upperby.

The handful of ex LNER namers on Canal sheds was just mystical. I so rarely saw them this early on. We also saw five of the ten Clan Class engines on that day, Nos. 72001/4/5/7/8, namely Clans Cameron, Macdonald, Macgregor, Mackintosh and Macleod.

I saw Pickersgill Class 3F No. 57653, which had already been withdrawn by the summer of 1962. I am surmising, from the way the numbers are grouped together, that it was on Kingmoor sheds, as was Princess Class No. 46200 The Princess Royal. There were Peak diesels on shed and in Citadel station and these were already working some trains over the Settle and Carlisle line.

I made two more visits to Carlisle during our time away, leaving Dad to enjoy his holiday with Mum and my sister in Grange. On the latter occasion I noted two Gresley Class J39s, Nos. 64888 and 64895, on 27/7/62, one at the beginning and one towards the end of the day. I wish I had been more specific in my note taking. It would have been helpful to have shed visits labelled as such, instead of little pen marks that occasionally offer hints of a change of venue.

Incidentally, on one of the few occasions when we were altogether and sitting outside a café in the middle of Grange, I saw someone fall off the mountain ahead of me. A group had been rock climbing, I think on Shepherd's Crag, or one close to it. Anyway, because I had seen the incident I was able to point the mountain rescue team to the spot, which otherwise looked like any other steep slope, partially hidden by trees. This was an age before the invention of mobile phones, of course. Good job I didn't go train spotting that day as well.

After only a week away this time, we were back at Penrith waiting for the train to take us home, which arrived behind Royal Scot Class No. 46159 The Royal Air Force. This would have pleased my dad, as he had served in the RAF during World War II. It is quite amazing how much traffic was around, during a relatively short journey homewards. Of note were unrebuilt Patriot Class No. 45507 Royal Tank Corps, Kitson Class 3F No. 47008, three Bowen-Cooke ex LNWR 0-8-0s and Gresley Class K3 No. 61969.

As soon as possible it was back to Crewe. Now I was actually dating my trips in my spotting note book. My fourteenth visit to Crewe on 1/8/62 obviously meant the same locomotives were cropping up with some regularity. Our response to this was total disdain. We were not alone. When Crewe based engines arrived at the station they could be met with a cacophony of jeering, wolf whistling or booing. We would refer to them as "crates", "stinks" or "relics".

This was quite the opposite to the reverential reception afforded, for example, to a Polmadie based Coronation, which might reasonably be expected at the head of the afternoon Glasgow to Birmingham express. This might be greeted with shreaks or yells of gratitude and appreciation, even waving, clapping and cheering. Quite what the train crews thought of this nonsense is anybody's guess. I suppose a large part of the travelling public were a bit mystified, as well.

Our disapproval of unpopular locally based engines went as far as inventing new names for them. The unfortunate Coronation Class No. 46254 City of Stoke on Trent became "City of Shit on Toast" and Britannia Class No. 70018 Flying Dutchman was heralded as the "Flying Dustbin". What wit.

That day at the beginning of August, we went out via Chester, where we saw County Class No. 1025 County of Radnor and Hall Class No. 6925 Hackness Hall and Castle Class No. 5088 Llanthony Abbey and another County Class No. 1011 County of Chester, appropriately, on the way back. In between there were seven Coronation Class representatives through Crewe, or in the sheds, including No. 46222 Queen Mary, which we saw less frequently than most. My first recorded visit to Wolverhampton Low Level on 4/8/62 was obviously a largely ex GWR affair. We simply spotted on the station for a few hours and came home, as we had gone out, via Shrewsbury. I recorded ten Castle Class and four King Class engines and I cabbed No. 6014 King Henry VII. The last of the Castles, No.7037 Swindon, was at Chester and only the fourth number recorded for the day. I have such a clear recollection of the moment.

She was in one of the centre roads in General station, facing Paddington, as it were. Waiting for her turn, she simmered whilst her crew busied themselves clanking around with the firing irons, in readiness for the task ahead. It was a typical event and one we must have witnessed so many times in a range of locations, but I remember her specially. Her name was so evocative of the GWR dynasty, the last of a distinguished line. There was something wonderfully unique about their big engines with their polished copper embellishments.

At the end of the same month of August the lads went to Preston for the day. I must have been at least partly attracted by the amount of Yorkshire to Blackpool and return holiday trains that crossed the main line at this junction station, including Jubilees and a K3, which I had seen on my way back from the Lakes.

The approach to the station by rail from the south was a long, straight section and it comprised at least a four track main line. From the platform end this meant it offered excellent opportunities to test your eye sight and your recognition skills of the different classes of engines as they approached from a distance.

The shape of their smoke deflectors was a give away for Brits, Semis and Scots. Scots and rebuilt Pates [Patriot Class] had curved ones and the slanted version on the Semis helped give them a seriously powerful overall bearing. We inaccurately referred to engines with smoke deflectors as having "winnies", short for wind shields.

Telling Jubilees and Black Fives apart from a distance was trickier. I seem to remember that the Jubilee smoke box door looked a little smaller, presumably because its boiler was a bit more tapered than the one on a Mickey [Black Five]. They also had a slightly more prominent metal shelf below the smoke box door, in some light conditions, which became more apparent as they got closer. I know, it's not very technical stuff, but that is how we did it.

If class recognition depended largely on familiarity and practice, quality of eye sight certainly came into it when it came to reading the digits. Initially, there was probably an element of competition to be the first to read the plate. It was very disappointing to me then, when it soon became obvious that Ian could read the numbers and shout them out when I could still only see a blur on the front number plate.

Luckily for me and without wishing to appear heartless, Ian's next door neighbour John, who joined us on that day at Preston, was hopeless. He could not read the front number plate at all and had to rely on the much larger cab side version, visible only as the train pulled into the station, much to our amusement.

Dad accompanied me on this trip to Gobowen on 28/9/62, as well. The purpose was to see King Class No. 6000 King George V passing at speed on a special train, travelling northwards towards Chester. This was asking a bit too much of my modest camera, once again.

Ian was a useful bloke to have around. In addition to his excellent eyesight, his mother always furnished him with coconut cake, when we went off together for the day. I mean a whole cake, freshly baked and still in its tin. It was sweet and gooey in the middle and crisp at the edges and we loved it. It gave us the short term energy we needed for our assaults on the sheds and the sometimes lengthy walks required to reach them.

Ian's mum was a star. She always referred to Ian as "Beany", on account of his being tall and thin. I spent a lot of time round at their house in the sixties. A very clever lady, perceptive and questioning, she always had an interesting angle on items in the news. She always saw the funny side of things, a trait which Ian inherited. She made me think, but when I referred jokingly to Ian as a "silly sod", she rebuked me very effectively. She also made an excellent cup of tea, into which I buried spoonfuls of sugar. She is the lone survivor of all our parents.

I must have had a very sweet tooth. My mum used to hide Penguin chocolate biscuits and the block of marzipan she used to ice the Christmas cake with, in her stocking drawer. As well as raiding the biscuits periodically, I would get a knife, carefully slice the end off the marzipan and then rewrap the bar to try to make it look as though it remained untouched.

I was permanently ravenous. On my return home from school each day I would start on two bowls of corn flakes, followed by two rounds of toast, left to cool before I spread the butter quite thickly and which were then washed down with a large mug of full-milk drinking chocolate [no such thing as semi-skimmed etc, then]. It provided a nice little appetiser before tea time. I had already cycled home in the middle of the day for a proper cooked lunch with a home made pudding. I was skinny as a rake, but I was always on the go. We all were.

That day at Preston I got the uncanny feeling that certain engines were starting to track my movements. Here was Britannia Class No. 70054 Dornoch Firth again and I wouldn't have been surprised if Jubilee Class No. 45574 India had followed me home. Oh yes and City of S. on T. on the Caledonian, for good measure! Occasional ex LNER engines offered interesting alternatives to the main fare, with Thompson B1 Class No. 61365 and Gresley K3 Class No. 61819 adding to the variety on the day.

Chester was still turning up its County Class examples on 18/8/62. Nos. 1022 County of Northampton and then 1013 County of Dorset were present at the start and finish of the day, with Castle Class. Nos. 7026 Tenby Castle and 5046 Earl Cawdor, sandwiched in between. Hall, Grange and Manor Classes all visited, in amongst a predominantly ex LMS and Standard list, which included seven Scots and Coronation Class No. 45256 Sir William A. Stanier F.R.S.

An interesting visitor to Birkenhead sheds on 21/8/62 was Class 4700 No. 4704, in the company of Grange Class No. 6870 Bodicote Grange and Class 2800 No. 3825. Three ex GWR types was probably as much as I ever saw together there. Only the day before I'd noted Patriot Class No. 45532 Illustrious and Hall Class No. 7903 Foremarke Hall in Birkenhead, possibly in Woodside, because they were the only two numbers I recorded for that date. I can't remember the circumstances and it will therefore remain a mystery and quite an occurrence, nevertheless. I can't account for it now, but there it is in front of me in blue and white, so it must be true.

I have never cheated when recording train numbers. I would only have been cheating myself. However, there were occasions when the overall feeling was that some one or other was telling porkies. One local spotter, for example, claimed to have seen Coronation Class No. 46248 City of Leeds in New Brighton station.

Firstly, I don't even know if that was possible from a loading gauge point of view. What I do know is that we did not believe him. If anyone knows differently nearly fifty years later it will certainly settle an old argument and I may yet have to eat humble pie. Spotters sometimes exaggerated in the same way as fishermen are supposed to. There was something to be gained from having a rarity turn up in your back yard, especially if you were the only one to see it, so I guess fabrication was tempting.

We went back to Crewe on 25/8/62, when the highlights included cabbing Royal Scot Class No. 46101 Royal Scots Grey. Cabbing was something we tried to do a lot, but more often than not it failed. Foot plate crews were often off-hand, but not usually rude to us, though the frequent requests by hordes of small boys to join them up there must have become quite a bind at times.

Cabbing gained you some credit in the story of the day, when told back home, to those spotting friends who, for whatever reason, had not joined you. The bigger and rarer the "namer" was, the better. The footplate was hot, noisy, and cramped, depending on how many of us had made it on board. The driver and firemen went about their tasks and we tried not to get in their way. Then they would say "Hop it" and that would be it and I would put a [C] next to the number in my book. An [H] in the notebook denoted hauled by and [P] stood for photographed.

On that particular day, the Royal Scot train was hauled by an English Electric Type 4 [what a boring name for a class we thought, although on reflection, slightly better than Hawker Siddeley Brush Type 4]. The Caledonian could only muster a Royal Scot Class No. 46129 The Scottish Horse and we saw the one off Standard Class 8P No.71000 Duke of Gloucester, which was not uncommon.

Royal Scot No. 46132 The King's Regiment, Liverpool was in Birkenhead sheds on our next visit, which was quite a turn up, though we did not get right round on that occasion, for some reason. The MPD foreman at Birkenhead must have got to know us pretty well. We always politely asked for permission and he almost always said yes. That was Sundays only though and we knew better than to try it on in the week. We had too good a thing going to spoil the unwritten arrangement. A week later we saw Hall Class No. 6990 Witherslack Hall on shed for the second time in seven days. She had become one of our regulars.

Our next trip to Preston on 15/9/62 revealed no diesels at all until we got off the train from Liverpool Exchange and even then there was only a handful of shunters in evidence, in addition to sporadic appearances from English Electric Type Fours on the main line Anglo-Scottish expresses. However, Preston was an excellent location for recording members of the Jubilee Class and we saw no fewer than twenty five of them on that day alone.

At the end of September I went with Dad to Gobowen, because King Class No. 6000 King George V was visiting on a special as far as Chester, which was unprecedented, in my experience. I thought there were route restriction issues with the Kings north of Shrewsbury. Anyway, it dashed through, bell first as it were, so that was mission accomplished. I guess Dad was invited along because I couldn't persuade any of my friends to join me. On the other hand it could have been because he was paying for the tickets.

On our way back home on 28/9/62 we changed trains at Chester, for Birkenhead. This enabled me to catch this shot of Royal Scot Class No. 46156 The South Wales Borderer, between duties at the north west end of Chester General station.

Chapter 3
1963

I was always short of cash. Money burnt a hole in my pocket. I just loved chips and sweets. As school boys we couldn't afford to go careering off by train all the time. We funded these exploits with our pocket money, with extra help from generous parents and some part time jobs, often short lived. I did a paper round and for a few months I sold Wall's Ice Cream.

We were taken from Port Sunlight in the back of a lorry and dropped off with our hand pushed trolleys, which were cooled inside with dry ice, into various Birkenhead housing estates and then picked up again at the end of the day. I have been reminded that on one occasion the front door was opened by Mandy Hill, who played on the wing for Tranmere Rovers. I remember that he had a particularly wide gait when he ran. I have possibly never seen a footballer since, whose legs were bandier than Mandy's were. That was as exciting as it got selling ice cream.

On one occasion I caught the edge of the kerb with my trolley wheels and sent a full load of choc-ices and Neapolitan family bricks all over the road. Another reason I did not stick it for long was that it impinged on weekend train spotting time.

The money I earned from my paper rounds, twelve of them a week, helped finance my trips, but only marginally. I earned ten shillings [50p today], in the form of a brown ten bob note, which was paid when we got back to the shop each Saturday morning. I promptly blew one shilling and one old penny of it on a large bottle of dandelion and burdock [10d] and a quarter of a pound of liquorice torpedoes [3d].

Britannia Class No. 70031 Byron brings in a Grand National special train to Aintree on 30/3/63.

I worked for Mr and Mrs J.H. Jones, a matchingly rotund, but jolly and kindly couple, who were the newsagents in our local parade in Mount Pleasant Road, where the whole neighbourhood did its daily shopping, prior to large scale domestic refrigeration and the supermarket revolution. When I started I was given the easiest paper round, displacing one of their stalwart and seasoned deliverers, who had obviously worked his way up to this most favoured position, closest to the shop.

Royal Scot Class No. 46156 The South Wales Borderer arrives at Aintree with the Tote Investors Grand National Special on 30/3/63.

I expected Jack's skivvy to give me a hard time after that but he never showed me any ill will. He just put his head down and got on with all the other little extra jobs that were heaped on him. He certainly "knew his place", in the way that complete subservience used to be described.

I suspect he was ousted for me either because they thought my parents were a bit posh or that I was a bit soft and it was quite possibly both. Mr Jones used to put his arms round my shoulders rather a lot, as if I needed a frequent squeeze of encouragement just to keep going. Simultaneously, some of his most trusted operatives were helping themselves to copious packets of cigarettes, on the other side of the stock room.

My round was the shortest and therefore the quickest. While my mate Ian was juggling with his sack and falling off his bike, cornering a steep hill at speed and sustaining some nasty cuts and bruises in the process at least a mile from the shop, I was back with my feet up and leafing through the comics.

Sunday papers, even more so today, of course, were stupidly heavy and required two separate trips. I wished everyone took the wafer thin Morning Star every day of the week, like the one communist on my round, who lived in Shiel Road. They were altogether more manageable, as newspapers went.

I started 1963 by visiting Chester again, on the 7th of January. There was just one County Class representative there this time, in the form of No.1019 County of Merioneth. In amongst the usual good mix of Western, London Midland and Standard engines was Stanier Class 5 No. 45110, going about her business and blissfully unaware of the star part she would play just five and a half years later, on the last day of steam on BR.

On 25/2/63 I went to Selby by myself on the green Trans–Pennine diesel multiple unit service with the curiously bulbous front end, which ran from Liverpool to Hull. I probably went on my own to get one over on the other lads. I think I chose Selby because the station was on the East Coast Main Line, well before the new diversion took the through line out of town and so in those days you could get there direct.

The first few months of 1963 were extremely cold. Though other parts of the country had it worse than we did, there was snow and ice on the ground for much longer than any year I can remember on Merseyside, before or since, though Mum told me 1947 had been a bit chilly too. It would have certainly seriously curtailed park football but it does not appear to have stopped me going train spotting.

Jubilee Class No. 45998 Basutoland marshalls empty stock from a Grand National special train at Aintree on 30/3/63.

It was definitely a very cold and foggy day in Selby, really rather surreal. Out of the mist came two Class A4s, Nos. 60026 Miles Beevor and 60006 Sir Ralph Wedgwood. The other highlights were Class A3 No. 60088 Book Law, Class A2 No. 60500 Edward Thompson and two Class A1s, Nos. 60151 Midlothian and 60144 King's Courier.

We were much more interested in named engines than ones without and we were even more interested in "namers" from other regions, as were being provided on that day. Overall, I had to admit that the ex LNER names were more exciting than our ex LMS ones. Regardless of the new additions I had collected, I felt Selby station was quite an inhospitable place, partly no doubt because I'd gone on my own, so I spent a lot of time in the buffet and I went home quite early. I've not been back.

On an undisclosed date, which I'm working out was probably early in 1963, Andy rang our door bell around tea time on a Sunday afternoon. He told me he had been to Edge Hill sheds earlier that day and seen Coronation Class No. 46245 City of London. He knew it was the only one of the class I had not seen, so this was a generous and noble act on his part.

That left me with a problem. It was school the next day and by the following weekend the Semi would have gone. It was a case of Dad to the rescue again. We went on the Sunday evening service by underground train to Liverpool James Street station, then by bus from the Pier Head along Smithdown Road as far as Tiverton Street and we walked past the terraced houses to the sheds. There she was, as promised, cold and hemmed in by other engines. I must have kept my part of the bargain with Dad, by not doing a full round of the sheds and agreeing to come straight home, because I have no record of the event. I had been the recipient of two good turns in one day.

Jubilee Class No. 45717 Dauntless and another member of the same class move off to Aintree sheds for servicing, having left their stock in sidings on Grand National Day, 30/3/63. These trains were generally packed with race goers, who had only a short walk from here to the course entrance. It took quite a time for the platform to empty of punters, once the special trains had disgorged their passengers.

Most of the special trains approached Aintree station from the south but this shot shows Royal Scot Class No. 46118 Royal Welch Fusilier arriving from the Ormskirk direction on 30/3/63.

Grand National Day at the end of March was damp and misty. All the race specials were steam hauled apart from one. Six Jubs turned up, including No. 45698 Mars, which I had recently seen at the buffer stops in Lime Street station and five Royal Scots. There were large and excited crowds milling around as the trains emptied and one notable visitor who stood out was an American Indian chief, in a full length head-dress.

On a trip to Ruabon on 20/4/63 I found just one Castle Class example, No. 7014 Caerhays Castle, but two Counties, Nos. 1027 County of Stafford and 1014 County of Glamorgan and three Manors Nos. 7806 Cockington Manor, 7827 Lydham Manor and 7819 Hinton Manor.

Rebuilt Patriot Class No. 45530 Sir Frank Ree pulls a special train into Aintree on the morning of the Grand National on 30/3/63. By early afternoon the specials had all arrived and we went home on the Mersey electric multiple units to watch the race on the television. The winning horse in 1963 was Ayala. We did not have a TV until 1964, so I no doubt went round to my friend John's house, to watch it on Grandstand.

On the 22/4/63 Birkenhead sheds held two of the Kitson Class 0F saddle tanks, Nos. 47005 and 47009 as well as ex LNER Class J94 No. 68065. The following week it had been joined by sister engine No. 68066 and I cabbed both. My guess is that they had been displaced from Bidston sheds on closure and were awaiting disposal themselves.

I noted that the new Western diesels had started to put in appearances at Crewe and even Chester, around this time. That was to be expected, as they were building them in Crewe Works and presumably running them in locally, but they also began to turn up on normal service trains out of Chester on Western Region diagrams, displacing Castle Class locomotives from the Paddington through workings in the process. Also at Chester on 1/6/63 was a Class B1 No. 61094, which was obviously lost. Though they must have got to Birkenhead sheds somehow and on a fairly regular basis, we hardly ever saw them in Chester General station.

In June 1963 my friend Mark and I went over the hills via Sheffield to Doncaster and York. We stayed at Bawtry and York youth hostels. A4 Class No. 60025 Falcon is seen approaching Bawtry viaduct, with its steel strengthened supports visible under the arches [4/6/63].

After my Selby sampler, the next big idea was an all out assault on the East Coast Main Line. This took the form of a mammoth three nights away youth hostelling venture, with friend and fellow spotter Mark, starting on 4/6/63. The itinerary was rail to Doncaster via Sheffield, bus to Bawtry youth hostel for two nights to allow a trip to Retford by bus on day two, returning to Doncaster on day three and by rail to York for that night, then home.

The youth hostel at Bawtry was handily placed within a few minutes walk of the town centre bus stops and the main line. The obvious location for spotting trains was from a swing park below the railway embankment. We received some very perplexed and curious looks from the local kids as we joined them for the evening, on what was clearly their patch. Gangs of youths can be very territorial, but we somehow managed to keep ourselves to ourselves satisfactorily and remained all in one piece.

My notes tell me I copped a total of 434 new numbers over the four days. Deltic Type 5 diesels were much in evidence, but there was still a lot of steam about. We saw four Class A4s on day one, including No. 60022 Mallard, but the moment I remember best was reserved for the evening, when we climbed the embankment at the north end of Bawtry viaduct and watched Class A1 No. 60157 Great Eastern, working hard towards Doncaster, presumably after a signal check. I remember the glow from the fire box, in the half light as she passed us. With that thought in our mind, off we went to bed in our mandatory sheet sleeping bags, in the men's dormitory.

Retford was well known, like Newark, for its diamond crossing and our visit was prior to its replacement by an underpass. Otherwise, Retford station was unremarkable but I copped Class A4 No. 60021 Wild Swan, so I was quite happy with it. On the bus journey we noticed that two girls had just been out to buy the new Beatles LP "Please Please Me" and they were waving it around excitedly, on their way home.

I was surprised to see only one "Streak" [Class A4] No. 60018 Sparrow Hawk on Doncaster sheds, but I did cop five more on the station, so I was not distraught. We were London Midland boys and this was all new to us.

In Doncaster station A3 Class No. 60054 Prince of Wales passes through on 4/6/63.

On to York and you could not fail to be impressed with the station itself. I still marvel at its grandeur today. I was still not making comprehensive notes. Trying to decipher exactly where the visit to the sheds was, from lines and squiggles, was never going to be ideal. I do not think we got right round and if we did there was certainly a lack of main line engines present.

There are also a few days in my spotting notebooks which look altogether threadbare, in terms of an apparent mismatch between venue visited and numbers taken down. These provide clues for alternative attractions, in other words occasions when trains were incidental additions to another event.

In the first week of June 1963 there are no numbers down in my book at all but I know that Ian and I went to Old Trafford Cricket Ground. I have no idea how we got there. Perhaps we went in the Tardis, which was already a popular means of transport by this time. Alternatively, I suppose it could have been a dad's car.

We bunked round Doncaster sheds and found A3 Class No. 60063 Isinglass veiled in its own smoke after a turn on 6/6/63.

I believe this was the first time I had watched live cricket at the highest level. That level was actually very high, as provided by the strong West Indies team of the day. We watched in awe as Wes Hall, Charlie Griffiths and Gary Sobers dismantled the England batting. Recent checks reminded me that the estimable Frank Worrell was playing that day as well.

Our trip to Crewe on 22/6/63 was notable for my second meeting with Coronation Class No. 46245 City of London. It was not unusual, having seen an engine you had been hoping would turn up for months, if not years, without success, that it would, once spotted, just keep on reappearing.

The next big trip was to Somerset, for our family holiday. We stayed at Home Farm in Curland, which was located six miles south of Taunton in the Blackdown Hills. Goodness knows how my folks found these places. They must have got hold of a guide to remote farmhouse holidays in inaccessible places. It was very rural and I remember Mum getting very animated by "'Til Death Us Do Part", or possibly "Steptoe and Son", or maybe it was both, on TV. We were without television at home at that time, but I think this experience swung it for me and my sister. They had also made a pet of a fox at this farm, which, I thought was a little offbeat, though very "sixties", I suppose.

I had a brand new note book for my numbers again and I temporarily upped my game for a time as far as neatness and organisation were concerned. Starting from Liverpool Lime Street, we were hauled by Bo-Bo Class B electric E3082 as far as Crewe, where Bo-Bo Type 2 diesel D5017 took over, then onwards through the Welsh Marches from Shrewsbury, by Castle Class No.4087 Cardigan Castle and finally from Bristol to Taunton, by Hymek Class No. D7017. North west to south west trains still went along the border route with Wales, rather than via Birmingham, at that time.

I wasted no time in getting in some serious spotting. From Taunton on the following Monday I went off to Exeter, behind Hall Class No. 4993 Dalton Hall. A quick spurt up the hill to Central from St David's behind Battle of Britain Class No. 34078 222 Squadron was followed by a trip out to Polsloe Bridge Halt, behind Standard Class 4 tank No. 80059.

Heaven awaited me at the end of a short walk. In fact, I'm pretty sure I must have run all the way there. I did a lot of spontaneous running between places. This was to be my first Southern sheds and Exmouth Junction did not disappoint. Well, actually that is a massive understatement. I was ecstatic. Fifteen Pacific cops, including one Merchant Navy Class, No.35026 Lamport and Holt Line. It didn't ever get much better than that. Back at St David's station, I cabbed West Country Class No. 34002 Salisbury and I was finally taken back to Taunton by Warship Class No. D866 Zebra.

On 1/8/63 Dad took me to the County Ground in Taunton, to watch a day of the Championship cricket match between Somerset and Nottinghamshire. I remember the name Brian Bolus and the wonderful setting, but not a lot else, though investigations remind me about another famous name from the past who was present that day, Fred Rumsey, the big Somerset fast bowler.

I spent three consecutive days on Taunton station. On the first of these I misjudged the exact location of the bus stop I was planning to alight at and I fell from the rear platform into the middle of the road, when the bus jerked forward, just beneath the bridge next to the station.

Undeterred by a shaking up and an odd cut and bruise, I scampered up to the station, sat on a platform bench and licked my wounds.

The following Saturday I saw thirty five different D800 Warship Class Type 4s, half the total. On the Western Region main line diesels were already firmly in control. My repeat visit to Exmouth Junction the following week yielded no less than five Merchant Navy Class locomotives.

On 8/8/63 I tried Bournemouth, though we went as a family on a day coach trip. Another member of the famous class of Pacifics, No. 35016 Elders Fyffes, was on the sheds, but it appears from my short list, that I did not get right round. Nevertheless, 441 cops for the holiday was not a bad haul.

My friends were also going on their own family holidays, of course and that could be quite uncomfortable for me, when they returned with stories of what they had seen on their travels. Ian came back from a fortnight in a caravan in Anstruther, having crossed the Forth Bridge at the same time that A4 Class No. 60012 Commonwealth of Australia was coming the other way. He had also been round St Margaret's sheds in Edinburgh and he had seen A3 Class No. 60077 The White Knight, amongst others. Inevitably, I never got to see either of them.

Back on our own patch, Birkenhead sheds was still bringing in things that I had not seen before, including ex LMS Class 4F No. 44309 on 18/8/63. Around this time also the shed code changed from 6C to 8H as part of a more widespread reclassification. At Chester on 26/8/63 we saw just one County Class No. 1016 County of Hants. I thought it a strange idea to use abbreviated versions of the county names on something as serious and important as a locomotive name plate. It didn't seem very reverential, somehow, but rather frivolous. No. 45552 Silver Jubilee, the first in the Jubilee Class came through, as did Coronation Class No. 46239 City of Chester, which of course seemed very fitting.

We cycled to Delamere Forest Youth Hostel via Chester on 5/9/63. This had been the first one we had stayed at, in April of the same year and it was the start of a new chapter in exploring the country. The hostel was deep in the forest, near a minor road and it was staffed by a very elderly gentleman warden. We were introduced to chores which were obligatory for hostel guests at that time. They ranged from washing up in the members' kitchen [Delamere and lots of others] to cleaning windows in a snow storm at St David's.

On a later date, I think at the hostel at Martham, the warden was demonstrating how to cut up some logs. He trod on a plank which held a nail facing upwards, which then skewered his foot, through his sandal. I think we were excused our duty on that occasion as he went off for repairs, having first pulled the piece of wood from his sole.

The line from Chester to Manchester went right past the hostel, but I remember that it was only lightly used, with vague recollections of the Stanier Class 8Fs and Ivatt Class 2s passing occasionally, on freight trains.

Also on Doncaster sheds on 6/6/63 was Britannia Class No. 70006 Robert Burns.

There were still namers to be found at Birkenhead sheds, including Jubilee Class No. 45583 Assam, which we cabbed on 13/10/63 and likewise Royal Scot Class No. 46118 Royal Welch Fusilier on 20/10/63, when Hall Class No. 6957 Norcliffe Hall was also present.

On 1/11/63 we set off for Birmingham on a school organised shed bash, round Bushbury, Oxley, Stafford Road, Tyseley, Saltley and Aston. How did we fit it all in? Talk about perpetual motion. We played football in the park, every single evening that the light permitted, as well. It's no wonder I was so thin.

We were very picky about the footballs we used. At the start we had to deal with "caseys", proper leather footballs with bladders inside. They were often not quite round in shape. They got very heavy when they got wet and it could hurt to head them, especially if you caught the laces which were tied up over the valve.

Luckily a new generation of realistic plastic footballs were being developed and we sampled a few different types. They had to fly right, during our training sessions. This was so we could replicate crosses, headers and saves in search of the perfect goal between the posts, or more accurately, between the tree and a jumper on the ground.

A great deal of careful experimentation had eventually taught us that this aim was much more likely to be achieved with a white plastic ball called a Frido Master 5, the flight of which could not be surpassed. Like all plastic balls, however, they were at the mercy of dogs with sharp teeth that were off their leads and we lost a few in this way over the years.

About this time we made a massive tactical switch of footballing venue from Earlston Park to Elleray Park. Factors relevant to this decision probably included:-

[a] The slope below Earlston Library was steep enough to be a nuisance, especially where it curled up in one corner.

[b] Complaints about the danger to the library windows from stray balls became too frequent.

[c] Dogs were taking no notice of the "dog run" sign attached to the railings on the adjacent disgusting parcel of land.

[d] Yet another failed re-seeding attempt by the corporation.

Elleray Park became our spiritual home for the rest of the 1960's, vying for the honour with Birkenhead sheds and Goodison Park. Elleray Park had better quality turf than Earlston, but had its own slope and some seriously misguided attempts to plant new saplings on what was obviously and even to the casual observer, going to be a necessary part of the pitch. We just played around them and amazingly they survived.

The only A4 Class on the sheds during our visit to Doncaster on 6/6/63 was No. 60018 Sparrow Hawk.

There was also a patch of shrubbery in the last third of the pitch at Elleray, to the right of the goal when kicking down hill. Spiky bushes posed a second threat to the new plastic balls, but footballers with malice could add insult to injury by timing slide tackles on the slope to perfection, so that the recipient ended up with a series of quite deep scratches from the thorns, in addition to losing possession of the ball. Grah made them his speciality, when he got fed up of being in goal.

Over the next few years we branched out a bit more on occasions, to Harrison Park, because it was actually flat and even further on, to an area on the other side of the electrified railway line between New Brighton and Wallasey Grove Road stations, which was really reclaimed beach, as a result of the 1930's construction of the King's Parade promenade. We knew it as the "dips" or the "sunken areas", as it was below the level of the promenade itself. Dave called it the "sun canarias", because he had a slight stammer and that made it sound altogether more exotic.

We spent so much time in the park we were even reluctant to leave when the park keeper came round on his bike to lock the gates. Sometimes we would go back in after dark and play "block-one-two-three", a derivation of hide and seek in which you had to get back to the base before being ticked by the person who was "on". We played a rougher version of this game, called British Bulldog, in the school playground. In addition to the seasonal obsession with conkers, such games were the mainstay of playground time for us as younger teenagers.

Generally, we kept on the right side of the uniformed park keepers, though we submitted them to a bit of banter from time to time. We did not do vandalism and they knew we were a pretty harmless lot. They tried to stop us fishing at the lake round the corner, known as the Captain's Pit.

This lake was stocked and protected by the local authority. It contained and I caught on occasions, gudgeon, rudd, roach, tench and perch; well, mostly gudgeon actually. There was also a large and famous mirror carp in there called Mabel. The stories about attempts to land her were legendary, but I was never convinced that she had succumbed to that indignity. There was a ritual stand off at the Pit as the "parkies" tried to stage surprise visits, appearing suddenly from behind a wall to catch us in the act. In response, we would pretend we were not fishing by standing on our reel of gut and trying to look like innocent bystanders. That did not always work and equipment did get confiscated from time to time. I fell into the Pit twice, once through the ice. Luckily, it was only a couple of feet deep, towards the edges at least.

Park football survived past the end of steam. We played with or against any one who turned up, except a group of lads from the catholic school, who mysteriously let it be known that they were "not allowed to play with us". Religious sectarianism was never an issue for us. Separate schooling left me a bit perplexed, but there was never any bother between us. By the end of the decade we had made two close friends who were Catholics. Yet, in Liverpool, it was still presumably a divisive matter, as there were councillors from the Liverpool Protestant Party representing certain wards in the city.

We ended up playing park football as men against boys. We showed them little mercy. When the youngsters wouldn't let us play with them any more because we were too big, Ian put the ball in the boot of his car and we played wherever we went. Often this ended up as a kick around in a car park, a habit we still have not yet entirely discarded, although we are now nearly all in our sixties.

Football kept us very fit for bunking round sheds, but on our November trip to Birmingham we had permits. We saw Castle Class No. 7001 Sir James Milne on Stafford Road, as well as sister engines Nos. 5026 Criccieth Castle, 7026 Tenby Castle and 5031 Totnes Castle. On Oxley sheds there were another two of the same class, Nos. 7024 Powis Castle and 5063 Earl Baldwin.

At Snow Hill, on the way home, I distinctly remember noticing Western Class diesel No. D1015, because it was in the experimental livery of "golden ochre", which should under no circumstances be confused with the "desert sand" of No. D1000 Western Enterprise, which was altogether different. We were quite happy with green and red for our big engines, thank you. Still, one hundred and fifty new cops for the day was a total not to be sniffed at.

What a fuss choice of liveries can cause today. I prefer to see engines just like they were in the sixties and exactly as I remember them. Therein lies the obvious nostalgia kick. Owners might reasonably have a different perspective and are not only entitled to do as they wish with their own machines, but I should consider myself darned lucky to have restored engines to look at in the first place.

There was once a Black Five which was wallpapered as part of an advertising campaign. That is where I draw the line. I would rather see Class A3 Flying Scotsman as No. 60103 and with German style smoke deflectors. I always thought they looked really cool, aided by the fact that there was no equivalent to these daring accoutrements on any LMR engines

I want them all to look like they do in Philip D. Hawkins' paintings. They are spot on. Malcolm Root is very good, too. On the other hand, pub signs, usually outside "The Railway", are notorious for messing up pictures of locomotives. Even some of the pictures I have seen for sale are hopelessly wrong in terms of their essential proportions. I'm surprised that the artists themselves can't see that. I guess it's because they are not always first and foremost train people. When you have stared at the real creatures as long as I have, you know instantly if the image is an accurate representation. They are just so familiar. Bird watchers call this the "gizz" of the bird, meaning the overall impression, the sum of its characteristics and movement.

Travelling by train was an important aspect of the day. To begin with, you had to be vigilant about trains approaching from the opposite direction, so someone had to be look out and that meant head out of the window and a high chance of smuts in the eye from your own locomotive. These could be painful and temporarily disabling. Some spotters wore goggles to fulfil this important task on behalf of their companions.

It was also a good idea to be up to speed about which side of the line sheds and stabling points were, en route, so that you maximised the chances of recording as many numbers as possible when passing.

AI Class No. 60128 Bongrace was spotted on Doncaster sheds earlier in the day before backing down light engine through the station [6/6/63].

I have never been able to concentrate sufficiently to wade through books on a train, though at home I was an avid reader. Earlston Public Library was on my way home from school and I used it a lot. I latched on to an author I liked and I would then read my way through their whole output, including The Secret Seven, The Famous Five, the William books, the Jennings series, Billy Bunter and Sherlock Holmes. My Dad tried to move me onto some more classical pieces, by buying me Kidnapped, by Robert Louis Stevenson, but I don't think I even opened the front cover. I knew what I liked and it wasn't too heavy.

Between Earlston Library and the "dog run" entrance to the park there were public toilets. We knew them well as a cottaging location, though that was not the word we used to describe what we imagined went on there. Though I never remember witnessing any thing untoward happening, it was certainly the case that some men spent an inordinately long time inside while we were just hanging around nearby.

The game we invented was to go as close as we dared to the entrance, yell "fruit in the bogs" and then leg it, in the hope that we escaped in one piece. I think we were actually mostly ignored by our intended victims, but it only took a rustling of paper or a sudden footstep from within to get the adrenalin going.

I have often thought since, with some sadness, that if it was true that homosexuals really had to meet in our suburban public loo, that they would not take our attitude to them as being homophobic. It is sobering to reflect that homosexuality itself was not de-criminalised in England until 1967. As with almost every other aspect of daily life at the time, our purpose was not based on malice and our only intention was to amuse ourselves. Adolescent boys are permanently out for a laugh, as any secondary school teacher knows, frequently to their own discomfort.

Another dimension to my parents' cultural awareness training programme was an offer to take my sister and me to see a D'Oyle Carte performance of the Gilbert and Sullivan light opera, The Pirates of Penzance, at Liverpool Empire. I thought it was fabulous, possibly much to my folks' surprise. A real orchestra, a visual feast and some catchy tunes, it became a regular fixture throughout the rest of the decade, whenever the touring company came to the city. It became a splendid family bonding event.

I was enjoying school more by now and attending more regularly. Much of this improvement I put down to getting on well with my peers. We had developed a good friendship group and although some joined us and some drifted away, the nucleus stayed the same. Partly it was geographical, in that we all came from the same area of the town. I heard it referred to as Upper Brighton, though I don't remember seeing that name in print or located on any old maps.

Our gang, as we have called ourselves for the last fifty years or so, even with the addition of girlfriends who eventually became wives, must have been a noticeable entity to those in our year at the grammar school, in spite of our being strung out across all four classes in the cohort.

We were never part of the sporting elite, who made up the first fifteen for rugby or the first eleven for cricket. If it had been football it might have been a different matter. Football was a working class game, played at the secondary modern school. We were not amongst the favoured academics, the eventual prefects, nor in the running for the victor ludorum title at sports day.

This V2 Class locomotive was passing through the station at Doncaster, southbound. Though the back of the print says 608xx, my notebook suggests No. 60886 was its likely identity [6/6/63].

We were not the chiselled featured, tanned, six footers, who had grown up quickly, had older friends and whose names were known around town, particularly at the girls' high school.

On the other hand, neither were we the swots, who devoted themselves totally to studying, regardless of their ability. We were neither bullies nor creeps. We were not even amongst the "divvies", our favourite word to describe the bland, the characterless and the socially inept. I thought about adding a lack of clothes sense to that list, but it felt a bit too close for comfort on a personal level. Nor, by definition, were we the loners or the ostracised. We were in the middle. I don't think any other group from school stuck together like we did, then or since.

Social awareness was very important at school. It was a bit of a jungle and as always, there were a few unsavoury individuals to circumnavigate. Playing them safely was a learned art. It involved not being confrontational, which actually came easy to me in physical terms, though I could be a bit mouthy. Being part of our group helped, as everyone knew we were friends. To keep on the right side of trouble makers, having a few tougher acquaintances, whose names we could mention in passing at appropriate times and who might, at a push, line up on our side or act as intermediaries, was probably useful too.

None of which was any help to me when I was out alone around the town. In my last year in the juniors I had been ambushed and imprisoned by an older boy in a makeshift den on a piece of waste ground that I passed every day on my way to school. Our town was littered with patches of waste ground.

On our journey back home from a family holiday in Somerset, our train, hauled by Warship Class Type 4 diesel hydraulic No. D845 Sprightly, passed two light engines just north of Pontypool Road station. Hall Class No. 4916 Crumlin Hall waits for its next northbound holiday Saturday commitment, just ahead of Britannia Class No. 70054 Dornoch Firth [10/8/63].

As a major city and sea port, Merseyside had suffered a lot from German bombing in the Second World War and although the mess had been cleared up, many of the spaces between the houses remained as unofficial playgrounds and increasingly, as time went by, they became unsupervised car parks.

On this first occasion, when I was ten years old, the local bully had made me drink sour milk from a grubby glass bottle and it was only when I started crying loudly that he thought better of it and released me. I ran home and planned an alternative route to school that I could use over the next few days.

I remember cycling to Birkenhead Woodside station to pick up the new summer timetable for the Western Region, with its chocolate brown cover. I was waylaid again, this time in the back streets of Birkenhead, by another lad on a bike. He was no doubt a bit bewildered by the timetable and he did not think it was worth taking off me, though I don't think we discussed its merits. He was more intent on thinking of an excuse to hit me. Eye contact was often considered to be sufficient provocation in these circumstances, as I had already discovered.

This was all in full view of a policeman on point duty, marshalling the traffic near Hamilton Square station. I managed to get away and made a beeline for the officer. He did not want to know, just motioning to me to go away and so I had to run the gauntlet again. It is amazing how fast I could cycle when I thought my life was at risk.

I felt more comfortable and safe on the trains than I sometimes did around town. When travelling by train I had to look out of the window. Otherwise I might have missed something. I liked watching landscapes go by and musing over what the people we passed were doing. There was something intriguing about viewing the different settlements, each with their own form and characteristics and all comfortably embedded within pastoral England's farms and woodland.

I felt reassured by the homely, orange glow of the urban street lights, as the train wound its way back westwards through small Pennine townships, on a cold, dark winter evening, while the under-seat heating burned the back of my calves.

We went round Llandudno Junction sheds on 2/11/63, cabbing Royal Scot Class No. 46148 The Manchester Regiment and recording a batch of the Standard Class 2 tanks Nos. 84001/3/9/20, which were used on the Conway Valley route to Blaenau Ffestiniog.

There were no fewer than three Class B1s on Birkenhead sheds on 24/11/63, which was a record for us. They included two namers, Nos. 61018 Gnu and 61189 Sir William Gray. Along with Hall Class No. 5939 Tangley Hall, that made for another milestone, with three named locomotives at the same time, which was never to be repeated.

Another school trip on 21/12/63 took us to Darlington, with permits for both sheds and works. Class A4 No. 60004 William Whitelaw was outside the workshops, minus its connecting rods. I saw a lot of engines that day, many of them out of steam, of course, but because it was new ground for us, it resulted in 190 cops.

We had a really good laugh on the lengthy train journeys that day, out and back on the Liverpool to Newcastle services, rabbiting away, teasing each other mercilessly, ducking in and out of the compartments of the coach, repeatedly opening and shutting the sliding doors. It must have been an absolute pain for other members of the public anywhere in the vicinity. I heard it said that one of our number actually threw a plate from the buffet out of the window in the general direction of a very main road during this trip, though I can barely imagine the consequences had it led to an accident.

I have it on good authority that the same person also once launched a snowball, which hit the driver of a DMU, through his open window, as it ran into Birmingham Snow Hill station and that he lit a banger on the Liverpool to Newcastle train mentioned above. I did not witness any of these events myself, but I am assured by others that the person in question is now a contrite, respected and law abiding member of his community.

On Christmas Day 1963 I received The Beatles album "With The Beatles", the one with the black and white cover picture of them in polo-neck sweaters. In order to make use of the twelve inch wide vinyl disc, I had a record player, which was almost certainly a model called a Dansette.

The turntable revolved at thirty three times a minute for the long players [LPs] and a switch could be thrown to speed it up to forty five revolutions to accommodate seven inch diameter singles, which it could deal with in multiple, through an ingenious release mechanism. For us, this was impressive technology. It provided us with an essential and seriously over used-piece of equipment and we all had them.

Forty fives, as they were often referred to, were an important currency of the day. You could gain status by taking new or sought after examples to parties, though you risked getting them scratched by careless users, or simply pinched. I left my collection at home.

Chapter 4
1964

The year began with Jubilee Class No. 45604 Ceylon on Birkenhead sheds on 6/1/64 and unusually, two sister engines together, Nos. 45579 Punjab and 455567 South Australia on 19/1/64. We went on to Crewe from there and saw The Duke [Standard Class 8P No 71000 Duke of Gloucester] again and Britannia Class No. 70000 Britannia, amongst the nine Brits on Crewe North sheds.

At the end of the month we did a shed bash in Manchester for the first time, through school. The highlight was probably the three B1s at Gorton. There were a lot of former LM locos around, though only a few namers and I copped 171 in total. We bunked round Edge Hill sheds on 15/2/64 and saw three adjacent Coronation Class Pacifics, Nos. 46233 Duchess of Sutherland, 46243 City of Lancaster and 46241 City of Edinburgh

Though this cloudy image is not dated, my note book tells me that I saw Jubilee Class No. 45661 Vernon on Birkenhead shed on 2/2/64 and that would seem to be about right for timing. Birkenhead sheds offered up occasional Granges, B1s and Jubilees amongst all the heavy freight engines.

By this time Ian and I were spending increasing amounts of time, usually on Friday evenings, in New Brighton, hanging around the stage door at the Tower. The Tower Ballroom, which was eventually lost to a fire in August 1969, was an important venue for up and coming groups, particularly those associated with the so called "Mersey Scene", also known as the "Mersey Sound".

We were usually the only youngsters there collecting autographs and we met members of The Searchers, The Big Three, Billy J. Kramer and The Dakotas, The Four Most, The Pretty Things, Wayne Fontana and The Mindbenders and The Merseybeats, amongst others. When we just missed Freddy and the Dreamers' arrival at the stage door Freddy's girlfriend took our autograph books in with her and sent them back to us through the post, with the all the band signed up. How nice was that?

Back on the trains and on our way to Crewe on 24/2/64 we saw Castle Class Nos. 5037 Monmouth Castle at Chester on the way out and 5055 Earl of Eldon on our return. This was the last time we saw members of the class in the city on normal service rosters on the Paddington expresses.

On 29/2/64, I've noted the numbers of one of the Western Region's "Blue Pullman" trains in Liverpool Lime Street station, presumably on a special. Though this particular experiment, with top and tail power units on express passenger trains, did not take off immediately, it presumably sowed the seeds that would eventually blossom in the 1970s, in the form of the Intercity 125 units.

A week later, on 7/3/64 we went to York and Leeds. Things were changing on the East Coast Main Line. We recorded plenty of V2s, B1s and some A1s, but there was a distinct lack of A3s and A4s, though I did manage to cab Class A3 No. 60070 Gladiateur on the station in York. At Farnley sheds, three Class A1s were withdrawn and in store, Nos. 60118 Archibald Sturrock, 60131 Osprey and 60134 Foxhunter. I seem to remember they were parked there for some time.

I only ever spent about an hour in total at Leeds Central station. It was not enough. I don't even know for sure exactly when I was there, as my notes do not give it away conclusively. It is possible it was on the same day as our 7/3/64 trip.

What I do know is that by the time I got there the Deltics had beaten me to it. I quite liked Deltics. Their impressive overall size and their high-set front windows and enormous snub noses gave them a certain authority, emphasised by a noisy and dirty vertical exhaust on take off. They kind of boomed out their presence, especially under an overall roof.

Leeds Central station still had some steam but the Gresley Pacifics were notable by their absence, at least in the brief time I was there. A whole list of these wonderful, old and long departed terminus stations that I visited comes to mind; Liverpool Central High Level, Liverpool Exchange, Bath Green Park, Birkenhead Woodside, and Manchester Central amongst them.

I still feel a definite sadness associated with the loss of edifices like these. Each one had its own atmosphere. I wish I had savoured them more and just sat for longer to take in their sights, sounds and smells. I was too fidgety to sit anywhere for long. It would have been more of a quick prowl around and then off to the next venue.

I returned to Bath Green Park just recently and enjoyed a lager in the bistro which occupies the main part of the old station building. I told the girl serving at the bar that I had last been there forty six years ago and she feigned polite interest. My wife and daughter motioned me outside to the tables spread out on the concourse before I bored her any longer and so I shared my reminiscences with them instead. They were rather drowned out, however, by the continuous clatter from the resident skate boarders. It is gratifying to find that at least some of these old cathedrals of steam have been saved and have been allocated new uses, Green Park serving as a regular market site in the daytime.

Sitting in the bistro with my family, I was reminded how different an experience the enjoyment of food has become, during the last half a century. Eating out is surely one of the great pleasures of modern life in cosmopolitan, multi cultural Britain.

Permanently hungry train spotters in the 1960s had a more limited choice. The alternative to fish and chips in our neighbourhood was the Chinese take away. We would overdose on carbohydrates with chicken fried rice and chips at Liu's, at the top of the hill, or get a fix of monosodium glutamate, in the form of chow mein and chips, or a tray of chips and gravy, at Tsang's, at the bottom.

Mr Liu used to entertain us with stories about exactly how far £5 would go in Lime Street, Liverpool, if you knew precisely where to go to spend it. Mrs Liu could not speak English and that was probably just as well. We must have been some of their best customers. Before long Ian and Grah were going to work full-time but were still living at home and so they suddenly had money for clothes and all sorts of other extravagancies, including, eventually, their own cars. Excess could be celebrated in a number of ways.

Grah, bizarrely, would buy a take away, eat a few mouthfuls and chuck the rest over the gate onto the girls' high school hockey pitch before going back to the shop for a replacement, just for the hell of it. It was our version of the Harry Enfield character yelling, "Look at my wad". John assures me rather belatedly and I think with tongue in cheek, that it was actually "performance art". I agree with him that it was hilarious.

On one or two occasions we were brave enough to try out that venue for a kick around. The grass surface was immaculate, but we spent so much time looking over our shoulders for caretakers or grounds men that it was difficult to relax sufficiently to concentrate on the footie.

This venue was adjacent to our local shopping parade in Mount Pleasant Road. Like all adolescents, we hung around for ages on street corners and particularly this one, next to the bus stop [numbers 7, 8 and 11], where the main road joined Kirkway and Mount Road and where we enjoyed close up views, therefore, of the revolutionary, new Atlantean buses, with the entrance at the front!

On 14/4/64 Battle Of Britain Class No. 34079 141 Squadron visited Crewe on a special train. This was the only time I saw Southern steam at the station. I was obviously so excited I was having trouble holding my camera steady.

"Lippy kids on the corner again......Do they know these days are golden?" sings Guy Garvey, in Elbow's nostalgic and moving rendition from their CD, "build a rocket boys!" We were only mildly lippy. We went through a brief phase of asking passers-by nonsense questions to elicit any sort of a response. "Excuse me, do you know the way to Mars, please?" was one or, "Have you got any white slime, please?"[instead of asking for the right time]. We were even polite when we were trying to be troublesome. A decision to walk only in straight lines, thereby involving clambering over cars and over garden walls did not last long either.

The year before last I revisited another old station after a very long gap, Manchester Victoria, starting point for our day out on the Cotton Mill Express circuit. I drove across the Pennines and was in dire need of the lavatory by the time I met the rest of the lads on the concourse. I ran, as fast as circumstances would allow, to the toilet. All the sit down facilities were locked up from the outside. It was probably the official response to some horrendous drug problem. I had to go as far as the excellent facilities at the nearby Arndale Centre. I can't remember ever being so pleased to see a large, modern, shopping complex.

We were in no need of such amenities when we did one of our annual early springtime, morning only, trips to meet the horse racing fraternity, on the other side of Liverpool. The Aintree Grand National special trains were mostly steam hauled again in 1964, though this time dominated by "Brits". Two Peak Type 4 diesels turned up as well.

We returned to Shrewsbury on 10/4/64. We were really into bunking sheds by now, not content to rely solely on school trips through the proper channels. Generally, this worked out well. We knew that we were trespassing and we generally had respect for and fear of authority. This added to the buzz we got from the experience. It was about as naughty as we got.

It was like a military operation, a quick surgical strike while the enemy's back was turned. It involved assessing the situation, noting the volumes of railway personnel then deciding on our preferred access points, as there might have been two or more to choose from. We assessed which entrance was least risky in terms of our being seen and also in relation to where we thought that most of the engines were likely to be located.

Then it was go, go, go. Once inside there was a permanently heightened sense of alertness. The adrenalin rush of avoiding confrontation and the thirst for numbers, combined with the potentially wonderful surprises that might be lurking in the deepest and least accessible recesses of the sheds, was a powerful stimulus.

We tended to hurry throughout, never totally relaxed, even after most numbers had been collected, or our presence had already been ignored by a few shed staff. There was always the chance of turning a corner and bumping into the foreman, in his trilby hat. If he saw us from a distance, he was likely just to shout at us to get out and we would, or at least we would make our way towards the exit, to reassess the situation.

If, however, we turned round a line of engines and virtually walked into him, he was more likely to give us a lengthy ear bashing and in the worst case scenario take us to his office and take names and addresses, as happened at Shrewsbury, though nothing came of it in the long run.

I can only remember being under suspicion from a policeman once and never from the railway police. He had observed us leaving the park over a wall rather than through the gate, so hardly a capital offence. He said to John, "What's your name?" "John Smith", said John, honestly. "I don't believe you", said the policeman. "Where do you work?" "We are still at school", replied John. "Show me your hands", demanded the policeman. We produced our out stretched palms. "Those are working hands", he insisted.

It was an unlikely conversation from an age where there was a more clearly cut class divide between us grammar school lads and those friends from junior school, who had had the misfortune to fail the eleven plus. With only one exception in our group, we were "grammar gogs". We spoke ourselves about lads of fifteen who had left school and found employment and had become "workies". Indeed, it was only a few years before that the minimum school leaving age had increased from fourteen to fifteen.

The inference the policeman was making was that our observed behaviour was not to be expected from grammar school boys but was more likely from "scallies", as we described naughty boys who had already left school and who happened to have manual jobs of some kind. The conversation went no further, but it was indicative of a heavily value laden technique for deciding whether some one needed further investigation or not.

There were very few scallies who made it to the grammar school. Indeed, it could largely be described as an intentionally scally-free zone. Corporal punishment was available there but not used much and the most subversive I can remember the clientele getting was when the free morning break milk bottle was replaced by a tetrahedron, with a plastic lining and a paper outer layer. For a short time they were discovered to be effective missiles, when launched from one end of the canteen to the other. The practice was stamped on pretty quickly [though not literally].

We bought frozen orange drinks in the same type of carton, called jubblies, which seemed to last for ages and gave you cold, orange lips and cheeks in the process.

Bunking round Shrewsbury sheds on our April trip, however, was worth the risk of a bit of bother. I copped Castle Class No. 7033 Hartlebury Castle on 10/4/64. After a night in the hostel we went back the next day and I copped sister engine, No. 5000 Launceston Castle, as well as Grange Class No. 6808 Beenham Grange and Modified Hall Class No. 7902 Eaton Mascot Hall. It was this second visit that had led to the altercation with the shed foreman.

This was part of a cycling and youth hostelling tour and there was quite a crowd of us. Twos and threes were probably best for bunking round sheds, rather than fives and sixes. We were a bit too visible on this occasion, with the other Mike and Brian, in addition to the usual contributors.

Over the border in North Wales there existed an intensive railway network on and around the Flintshire coalfield. I never explored the area satisfactorily but I recall certain aspects that I wish I had found more time for. The line from Chester General to Mold, Denbigh and Ruthin was still operating in the early 1960s, though it was an early casualty of the cuts. I remember that Ivatt Class 2s were used on some of these services.

There were also lines to the quaintly named Brymbo and Minera, up in the hills, west of Wrexham. Brymbo still had an operating steelworks and we saw freight on this stretch occasionally, although it was always from a car, during a weekend drive into the country.

On 16/5/64 I made my first of two visits to Caergwrle Castle and Wells. This was a scenic spot for a day out and it could be reached directly by diesel multiple unit on the New Brighton to Wrexham service, which later only came in to Wirral as far as Bidston, presumably to prevent it getting entangled with those provided by the Mersey underground EMUs.

We took a picnic and I copped 5600 Class tank No. 5667 and 5700 Class Tank No. 9608, both passing through Caergwrle with short freight trains. We walked up to the castle and had an unusually relaxing day.

On 12/7/64 Ian, Mark and I did something we had not done before, namely we joined in with a railtour of South Wales sheds organised by the Warwickshire Railway Society, which we met up with at Crewe. I can't remember the exact timings, but I'm pretty sure it involved a very early start for us. It took us round Worcester, Hereford, Pontypool Road, Cardiff Canton, and Severn Tunnel Junction sheds and I eventually counted 197 cops. We were hauled by Castle Class No. 5054 Earl of Ducie and A1 Class No. 60114 W.P.Allen, which disgraced itself by failing, I think at Worcester, on the way back home.

After we had been returned to Crewe and waiting for a late train back to Liverpool, I went to sleep on the bench outside the buffet. When it was time to get on the train, Ian and Mark could not wake me up. I was out for the count. I could not manage a second consecutive night without sleep. They were obviously concerned, but an off duty nurse assured them I was simply exhausted. They literally carried me home. I woke up in my own bed, at mid-day the next day. I have never felt so disorientated in my life. I should have still been on Crewe station. I might have missed some numbers on the way back.

On the way to Chester on 27/6/64 we called in at Mold Junction sheds to find Jubilee Class No. 45657 Tyrwitt in the company of Grange Class No. 6831 Bearley Grange. Two more Jubilees passed through Chester that day, while we were there, Nos. 45633 Aden and 45600 Bermuda. The only other namer to put in an appearance was Britannia Class No. 70046 Anzac.

It was soon holiday time again. Back to Somerset, this time with a week each at farmhouses in Stoke-St-Michael and Farmborough. This time I was allowed to take my bike. On reflection, that was a good move. My Mum and Dad seemed to like more out of the way places, as representing more of a contrast, no doubt, to our very built up home environment.

I had a brand new spotting note book, my fourth one in the series of six that I still possess, so again, the numbers look quite presentable for the first few pages. What a sense of freedom a bike gives you. I still feel liberated, when I get on my bike today, but on that occasion it simply meant I could get more easily to the places I really needed to be.

At the end of our journey to Bath via Bristol, I went straight to Bath Green Park sheds. I was aware of the esteem in which the Somerset and Dorset railway was held by enthusiasts and I was keen to enjoy some of it myself. Two of the S.& D. Fowler Class 7Fs were on shed, Nos. 53807 and 53809. That was a magic moment.

A day or two later I went back to Bristol for Barrow Road sheds, on the look out for unusual Jubilees that generally bypassed us Crewe lads, but I only saw Nos. 45641 Sandwich and 45608 Gibraltar, both of which I'd seen before. The Western Region Main Line seemed to be all diesels. Next time out, at Swindon, I copped Western Class 4 diesel No. D1000 Western Enterprise, amongst others.

I also got to Gloucester, Exeter, Newport, Cardiff and to Dai Woodham's Barry scrap yard for the first time, where I copped nearly everything I saw. I like to think that I cycled each time into Bath to start the day off, but on reflection, maybe I went in on the bus, sometimes. I was brave enough to bunk round sheds on my own now, single-minded in my pursuit of yet more numbers.

The day that stands out for me still, was on 3/8/64, when I cycled to Templecombe. It was a warm, sunny day and as I turned into the station approach road, which was on a bit of a hill, I was panting a bit. Wafting out of a window from a nearby cottage came Manfred Mann's "Do Wah Diddy Diddy". I can hear it now, as if it was yesterday. "There she was just a walking down the street, singing….."

It appears I did not attempt to get round the sheds, contenting myself with the largely Southern fare on the main line. If the choice was ever between big, green named engines and smaller, black unnamed engines there was no contest. I saw three Merchant Navy Class representatives that were new to me, Nos. 35014 Nederland Line, 35028 Clan Line and 35006 Peninsular and Oriental S.N. Co and so my decision not to concentrate on the S. & D. section was justified.

I went to Weymouth on 4/8/64 and Eastleigh the next day. I somehow managed to get round the works here, where the highlight would have been Merchant Navy Class No. 35007 Aberdeen Commonwealth. I remember being intrigued by the curious design of the Q1 Class, with members in the works and on the sheds.

The journey home was special, because it was the only journey I ever took on the old Somerset and Dorset. I cycled to Radstock, rolled my bike into the green brake van and was hauled to Bath Green Park by Standard Class 5 No. 73054. If I could have my time again…….. Anyway, I mustn't grumble. I copped 690 on the holiday and for me then, that was still what it was all about.

If numbers were the driving force, then location, location, location became even more important. Standing on a busy station, watching the comings and goings, provided the archetypal image of the train spotter and that could be enjoyable beyond belief. Incidentally, the term gricer, used to describe a train spotter, is one I have only ever read about. Strangely, I have never heard it in conversation, nor did we ever use it at the time on the platform ends.

Sheds and works were where the sheer volumes of numbers congregated, so they had become the focal point of our activities very early on. Turning up at the sheds without a permit, we were faced with a permanent dilemma; do we ask or do we bunk round? There were places, like Crewe North, where asking was a complete waste of time. It was too busy and they would have been even more inundated with small boys than they actually were. We got kicked out regularly from a number of sheds, including Crewe North, which we accessed through gaps in the railings at the far end of the shed yard, as well as from Crewe South and Carlisle Kingmoor.

On Sundays, chances were enhanced, because the sheds themselves were quieter, with fewer staff around. Asking permission sometimes worked, where shed access itself was limited and took you past or close to the foreman's office. Later, as the end of the steam era approached, it appeared that attitudes became a lot more relaxed.

This could be interpreted, of course, as railway personnel losing faith in their own business and pride in their work. This might have then manifested itself as indifference to our presence.

In any event, by the mid 60s, we were no longer relying solely on school for permits, nor were we always leaving it to chance and I remember writing off for them myself. Generally, we found that works were comparatively impenetrable, without a pass. I think it was sometimes possible to turn up at the main entrance at Crewe Works, pay a small fee and attach yourself to other parties of youngsters, who had already made arrangements to go round, but I might have dreamt this.

On the less than helpful day of 22/4/64, [weatherwise, that is] a Stanier Class 8F takes the Crewe station avoiding lines, which disappeared down into a burrowing underpass, beneath the main lines at the north end of the station. It was apparently too dismal a scene even to get the number. This line could only be viewed from the bottom of the footbridge which led to Crewe North depot and was really out of bounds to us. It was known to us as the "Muck Hole". This was quite an appropriate name, as it dealt exclusively with freight traffic and after a train had passed though it carried on emitting smoke for a good long time.

The elderly railway employees, entrusted with the health and safety of getting on for a hundred over excited kids in a massive engineering concern, where hazards lurked around each corner, actually often turned out to be rather blasé in the end, as well as co-operative and informative. The guides wore dark blue rain coats and hats with shiny peaks. We got to recognise them and one shorter gentleman reminded me of the comedian, Arthur Askey. Perhaps, for their part, it was more a case of, "Not you lot again."

When the gates opened there was inevitably a bit of a scrum, despite the barked instructions from the guides. I think we might have tried to slide ourselves in through the melee once or twice, but if so, it was an impromptu event rather than regular policy. Set times for trips round the bigger works might have made this a more attractive ploy.

On 13/8/64 Brian and I went to London, staying in youth hostels at Holland House and Earls Court. This youth hostelling lark had become very important for us. We even did walking and cycling breaks in the Lake District, which did not involve trains at all for days, though we would usually try to fit Carlisle in at some stage. It was sociable, relatively cheap and it certainly helped us get around. There were also girls there and by now that was a big plus. The hostels opened at 5.00 p.m. and the tactics were to get in quick, check in at the warden's office, have a cursory wash, make up your bed and then search the place for talent, as we then referred to the opposite sex.

My wife has insisted, as the price I have had to pay for her co-operation in looking through my draft, that I might have been more successful on such occasions, if I had made time for a proper wash and a change of clothes.

The members' kitchen was a definite hot spot. Competitive male egos then took over and normally amicable friendships were temporarily at risk, as some fairly basic instincts helped establish that evening's pecking order. That depended to an extent, of course, on how we had been received by the objects of all the attention, which was far from favourably in some instances. I will gloss over much of what followed. It is not the time or the place. Suffice it to say, that a scoring system of sorts was involved, but it was all, inevitably, pretty innocent stuff in the end.

I became a good customer of the YHA. I stayed in 134 different hostels in Britain and Europe between 1963 and 1975. I met a lot of interesting people and it allowed me to get to see places I would otherwise not have been able to afford to visit. As the sixties progressed we rather misinterpreted one of the main maxims of the organisation, which was travelling under your own power.

Later on, as the first couple of the lads passed their driving tests, aged 17 and indeed started to buy their own cars because they had left school for full-time jobs, the temptation to stay in hostels and travel by car was too great, so to a degree, we ended up abusing the system.

We used to joke about travelling by canoe, but we never fooled anyone and the wardens often turned a blind eye to it. Soon afterwards, of course, the organisation itself went through a lot of soul searching about its own identity and raison d'etre, before adapting to the social changes that were taking place.

Anyway, with Brian in 1964 it was still very much a train spotting trip. My note book is unhelpful about where we went except when we got to the sheds. We went round eleven installations in and around the capital, spending the rest of the time on the main line stations and at Clapham Junction. I copped 573 locomotives. It was a good job done, though I can't remember any particular highlights.

As the scrapping rates of steam engines picked up, their diesel replacements were becoming much more common and from the lists I made, it appears it was only the Southern Region, and more particularly the ex LSWR main line out of Waterloo, where steam truly still ruled.

After an early trip out to Norwood Junction sheds, which turned out to be a bit of a wild goose chase anyway, we did take the rest of the day off to go to see some cricket at the Oval. It was eventually a draw against Australia, but not before Colin Cowdrey and Ken Barrington had made the game safe for England, by batting through a large chunk of day four of the test.

We went to Derby on 4/10/64 and visited Burton sheds, which still had a lot of ex-LMS steam, but the changes were clear now and we knew we had to target areas a bit more carefully, if it was steam we were primarily after. The only namers we saw that day were five Jubilees, only one of which was a cop, No. 45620 North Borneo.

The general election of October 1964 was the first I remember taking an active interest in. The reason was that my parents were committed Labour voters, having first met in the Labour Club at Liverpool University in the late 1920s. As was no doubt the case in many families, my own views of the world were fashioned in my teens by listening to my parents' discussion and then gradually chipping in myself.

In our middle class, suburban part of Wallasey we were pretty much surrounded by our political adversaries. I relished that, as it appealed to my competitive and argumentative instinct. Dad was in administrative social work with a regional charity. Four of us lived on his modest wage, as my Mum was a full time and devoted house wife and mother. She was also a well qualified former Head of English in a girls' grammar school. After 1965, humble, kind and dutiful as she was, she additionally became a full-time and long-term carer to her sister, who suffered from schizophrenia.

During the October half term holiday we were back in the Lakes, doing Carnforth sheds on the way up, staying at Carlisle youth hostel overnight and from there dipping into Kingmoor and Upperby. Class A3 No. 60041 Salmon Trout was a cop on Kingmoor, presumably after the closure of Carlisle Canal. Class A4 No.60027 Merlin was also present.

At Upperby, the next day, I recorded no less than six Coronation Pacifics in a row and stored out of service, alongside the main shed buildings and if it had not dawned on us already, we could see it now in front of our eyes. The writing was on the wall for the railway as we had known it and our favourite big engines were not immune.

Luckily there were other distractions. We had started going to parties by this time. This basically meant persuading somebody's parents to allow us the use of their lounge for an evening, with licence to play the record player more loudly than usual.

Then it was a matter of hoping to find some girls to invite and praying they would accept the invitation. This was not quite as straightforward as it sounded, because we went to a single sex grammar school and only at youth club and badminton club did we mix spontaneously with the opposite sex.

We had another Somerset family holiday in the summer of 1964. On the journey home Standard Class 9F No. 92000, with what looks like a serious lime scale problem, backs down onto its train at Bristol Temple Meads station on 8/8/64. As our train left, so too did the Standard, running parallel with us for a time through the Bristol suburbs. This sort of simultaneous departure on a four track main line was, of course, relatively rare. The only other instance I can remember witnessing it was when our approach to York from Leeds coincided with that of A3 Class No. 60036 Colombo on the down main line, after Church Fenton. This was also a particularly stimulating sight, to see the motion at work close up and to hear the engine working hard provided fabulous memories.

Brian's brilliant Mum was one of the first grown ups to relent. She was a vivacious lady, always beaming, friendly and welcoming. She went a step further by asking her hair dresser's daughter to bring her girl friends along to a little get together in their first floor flat. I already really liked Brian's Mum a lot. She worked at the Cadbury's factory in Moreton and regularly brought home big bags of broken chocolate biscuits, for us to gorge ourselves on.

This first party started a whole series of liaisons between our gang of lads and various friendship groups of girls in the area, including, at different times, Oldershaw Girls High School, Maris Stella Catholic Girls High School and Birkenhead High School for Girls, as well as two lots from Wallasey High School. The date for our first ever proper party was 5th December 1964.

I met Pauline that night and she became my first girlfriend. I took her to see Goldfinger at the Gaumont cinema in Seacombe and A Midsummer Night's Dream in Liverpool during the following months, because it was one of her set books for English Literature "O" level exam. I went round to her house on Saturday evenings and we listened to her P.J. Proby records and I tried to get her to like the Animals and the Beach Boys. Her Mum and Dad kept popping into the lounge to make sure we were "all right". I got off on the wrong foot by breaking a ceramic figurine that stood on their window sill. Trains temporarily slipped from the top of the agenda, but as it turned out, not for long.

Chapter 5
1965

It was two and a half months before I went train spotting again, after an unproductive visit to Chester between Christmas and New Year. I was obviously a bit preoccupied. My first big trip in 1965 was to go to Leeds and Hull on the 6th of March. Why Hull I have no idea, except that I had never been there before, which, of course, is actually quite a good reason to visit a place. On the way there was a clutch of Jubilees on Holbeck sheds, in the company of Britanna Class No. 70040 Clive of India.

We were back at Aintree for Grand National Day in 1965, to see Ivatt Class 2 No. 46444 approaching the station from the Liverpool direction. The date is 27/3/65.

Back at home and prior to our owning a TV, the radio was a very important source of entertainment. I made a point of listening regularly to some of the half hour long comedy shows. My favourites were the long running "Clitheroe Kid", with Jimmy Clitheroe and from 1965, "Round the Horne", starring Kenneth Horne.

The critical station for us, however, was not on the BBC, but Radio Luxembourg on the medium wave band. The only advertisement I remember it running was for the Horace Bachelor Infra Draw method for completing football pools coupons, which was based in Keynsham between Bristol and Bath and which we were constantly reminded, was spelt K-e-y-n-s-h-a-m. They certainly played that one a lot. I found out later they made Fry's Chocolate Cream in that town as well, which would have been rather more appealing to me than betting.

Stanier Class 5 No. 44778 stands at the platform waiting for the peg, as we described signals at go, having brought in a Grand National special train on 27/3/65. The engines in this class were always either "Mickeys" or "Black Fives" to us.

Radio Luxembourg was only available in the evening and suffered from generally poor reception, which became more obscured by the output from other stations the later into the night we persevered with it. Nevertheless, it was initially a lifeline, which allowed us to keep abreast of the pop music revolution.

In 1964, the pirate radio ship Radio Caroline had taken to the waves and parked itself near to the Isle of Man in the Irish Sea, to make its rebellious contribution to the swinging sixties. We soon identified with it as our radio station. It was relatively short-lived, however, as the government moved in and sank it, figuratively speaking and we were eventually catered for by the more sanitised BBC version, Radio 1.

By this time my sister and I had consistently harangued my folks so much about not having a telly that they had given in. This opened up new horizons for us, in the form of Juke Box Jury and Ready Steady Go. The former was well established by then, to the extent that I had already sat on a panel copying the programme's format after school one day, to pronounce on the latest releases.

Britannia Class No. 70052 Firth of Tay arrives at Aintree on 27/3/65.

I have no idea why I was asked to take part, other than I suppose I was prepared to speak my mind. I made unflattering noises about the Rolling Stones latest number and was virtually booed off the stage. I think I felt honour bound to support the Beatles in their supposed rivalry with the Stones, though it may actually have been a bit too early for that.

On 13/4/65 we ended up at Swindon, as the furthest point on what was nominally a cycling tour from home to the Cotswolds. Riding on average between fifty and sixty miles a day and using mostly main "A" class roads, Rick and I did not complete the whole itinerary. We hitched a lift in a tip up truck when we felt a bit tired, somewhere in Warwickshire. The bikes went in the back and we sat up front next to the driver. It was a mistake that the other six cyclists never ever let us forget.

Quite a coincidence, but virtually the next train in, under the road bridge at the Liverpool end of Aintree station on 27/3/65 is sister engine, Britannia Class No. 70051 Firth of Forth. For reasons unknown, this is recorded on the back of the photo itself, but not in my record of the day, in my note book. I then went home to watch Jay Trump win the Grand National-on our own telly! It had an X-shaped aerial, spindly legs and a fuzzy picture, but it was our telly.

On the way south we stayed at Stratford-Upon-Avon and in one of those bizarre and random moments of our youth, we called at the door of a house where we had been told that Rolf Harris lived. There was no reply. Probably just as well. I didn't even like Rolf Harris's stuff.

Funny how, eventually, we always seemed to gravitate towards the railway, even when, as on this occasion, not everyone involved was interested in trains. I copped Hall Class No. 6927 Lilford Hall on Oxford sheds and at the same venue on the next day, sister engine No. 6956 Mottram Hall. In amongst the Halls, Prairies and Granges were two Britannia Class engines, No. 70051 Firth of Forth on the first visit and No. 70000 Britannia on the second.

Our social calendar in Wallasey was picking up nicely through out this period. We had started to attend a couple of youth clubs, those attached to churches in the area and they had started to attract live music, associated with the explosion of young bands on Merseyside at the time. Even our school got in on the act, holding end of term dances in the main school hall. We were treated to The Undertakers, Earl Royce and The Olympics, The Calderstones and The Bumblies [later The Crying Shames, favourites of ours who had a minor but memorable hit record, called "Please Stay"].

In April 1965 a group of eight lads went on a mammoth bike ride staying in youth hostels and getting as far as the Cotswolds. The only photo of trains I took while we were away was West Country Class No. 34040 Crewkerne standing in Oxford station [15/4/65].

On 5/6/65 I went by train to Manchester with Ian and then to Old Trafford Cricket Ground for the first day of the Roses match between Lancashire and Yorkshire. We were there in good time and noticed Geoffrey Boycott, in his pads and leaning on his bat. He had just finished having a net practice and was deep in conversation with the off spinner Don Wilson and another man.

We went up to them and eavesdropped, effectively completing a circle of five. They carried on chatting and totally ignored us. After our fix of adulation we saw Fred Trueman open the bowling, eventually taking three wickets for twenty three runs. Boycott's early morning net was not wasted. He was thirty one not out by the close of play.

We played a lot of park cricket ourselves in the summer, alternating with football which had no close season. When the weather was fine for a time the park was dry and the ground was often bone hard, under a thin sandy, surface layer. It was difficult to knock the stumps into, so we sometimes used the base of a tree instead. Enter another friend and neighbour, Peter, who was not a train spotter for some reason, but who did have his own set of stumps, which were fixed onto a solid wooden block.

Peter had a quiff and a fast walk and he saw himself as an elegant batsman, with some exaggerated extra flourishes of the wrist when striking the ball. If things did not eventually go his way, he was quite capable of sweeping his fringe over his ears, sweeping his stumps under his arm and beating a sudden and hasty retreat. Then it was game over and back to football.

This was the only photograph I took on my first trip to Barry, probably because it was a namer. We definitely had a bit of a thing about namers, whatever their condition. It shows Merchant Navy Class No. 35025 Brocklebank Line in Dai Woodham's scrapyard on 24/4/65.

Pulling away from the North end of Crewe station on 25/6/65 is Britannia Class No. 70019 Lightning.

In spite of these competing demands on our time and resources, we kept up our interest in trains by next visiting South Wales on 24 and 25/6/65. Canton sheds was all diesel, although Newport still had some ex GWR steam, as did Cardiff East Dock. I copped two namers there, Modified Hall Class No. 7925 Westol Hall and Manor Class No.7804 Baydon Manor. Just outside Cardiff Queen Street station we saw Standard Class 9F No. 92220 Evening Star, in steam. I didn't cop a thing on the Barry scrap lines, because I'd been there the previous summer, but I suppose that was missing the point a bit, in a way. It was more of a pilgrimage. Although most Barry detainees were eventually saved for the preservation movement to come, I believe they did get round to scrapping some engines early on, including the only Warship Class diesel I never saw, No. D600 Active.

Birkenhead sheds could still put on a good show and I copped eight on there on 3/7/65 and another four a fortnight afterwards. This was the prelude to our family holidays, which in 1965, as you will have guessed, we took in Somerset, though perilously close to the border with Dorset. The precise location was Axe Farm, near Crewkerne.

Warship Class diesel No. D817 Foxhound is bound for London Waterloo on the former LSWR main line at Clapton near the Somerset and Dorset border on 25/7/65.

On the evening of 25/7/65 at Clapton Crossing near Crewkerne, on the Exeter to Waterloo main line, daylight is rapidly fading. I had reason to believe that the Plymouth to Brighton train might still be steam hauled. The signal man kindly phoned a colleague further west to check, but the train was late and the wait continued. Eventually I heard the bells in the cabin as the train entered the section, followed by the magical sound that always gave us a tingle, the rhythmic beat of the approaching steam engine. The headlamps of West Country Class No. 34005 Barnstaple arrived through the gloom, at last. Nice story, sorry about the picture.

Our journey was memorable for two reasons. Firstly, Ian and his family were going on holiday to Weymouth on the same day, so we could share our hobby as normal, en route. Secondly, we were all travelling via London and on to Waterloo. Ian and I took a walk round Soho at lunch time and in Greek Street we bumped into Allan Clarke, lead singer of The Hollies, who gave us his autograph. Ian and his folks took a different [steam hauled] train to the west from Waterloo, while ours departed behind Warship Class No. D815 Druid.

Our holiday location was handy for the ex LSWR route from Waterloo to Exeter and the nearest point to the farm was at Clapton, where a manned signal box controlled a modest level crossing, on a pretty quiet minor road. Since singled, this was then still very much a double track main line, although diesels, in the form of the Warship Class, had taken over all the London expresses.

A diesel interlude, which I recognise is a little out of keeping with the theme of the book, but I quite liked the Western Region examples, particularly. Hymek Class No. D7027 is at the main down platform at Exeter St David's station on 31/7/65.

No bike this time, but I got around a bit by bus and train to Weymouth, Bournemouth, Newton Abbott, Exeter, and Plymouth, all on different days. I also got back to Templecombe and this time I went round the sheds. It was very quiet. There were sixteen steam locomotives on shed, from ex GWR, ex LMS and Standard classes. All those I copped were Ivatt Class 2 tanks.

Hymek Class diesel No. D7033 pulls out of Exeter St David's station in the direction of Plymouth on the 31/7/65.

Templecombe was a wonderful location, combining main line with cross country so effectively. Later on, I obtained a sound recording of S. and D. locomotives at work, which included some very evocative station announcements that reminded me of its charms. I liked station announcers per se. In the 1960s they sounded so official and important. You got the impression as a youngster that this was a top job, really prized, as though they sat there controlling the flow of traffic through their microphone, the all important fat controllers.

There were some lovely regional accents on the smaller stations in contrast, no doubt, to the Queen's English being delivered at the London termini. They often seemed to take real care over pronunciation and delivery. I would listen attentively to the long list of stations the train would visit and try to memorise them in order.

On my record the announcer's voice was heralded by a sharp click or electrical scratch, as the public address system was turned on. "Templecombe, this is Templecombe. Change here for Bath and Bournemouth lines". This was the background accompaniment for what sounded like a very abrupt stop at the down main line platform for an express from Waterloo. I imagine it was hauled by a Bulleid Pacific. Open doors were rapidly slammed shut as the station staff did their best to get the train restarted to regain lost time. I played it time and time again. It brought it all back.

At the end of the family holiday Mum and Dad went home to look after my aunty, who was going to come to live with us. My sister and I proceeded to Winchester to stay with our uncle. I just carried on spotting. I do not have a clue about how my sister spent her week, other than that she was not present at all on Winchester station, but she did buy Tom Jones's number one single hit record, "It's not Unusual", while we were away. Perhaps that was her comment on my single-mindedness.

Western Class diesel No. D1039 Western King stands at Exeter St David's station with a south west bound express on 31/7/65.

In addition to the many hours I spent on the down platform there, I visited Portsmouth and Southampton. Again, I got round the sheds and somehow the works too, at Eastleigh. By this time I needed only one Merchant Navy Class No. 35020 Bibby Line, to have seen them all. I think I must have had a tip off, anyway, there it was in Eastleigh Works in the process of being broken up. Her number, 35020, was chalked onto some of the bigger pieces that were strewn around the place. I'm afraid I just had to count it to "class" my Merchants, though I wake up in the night about it still. Cold sweats, guilt ridden, did I cheat?

Saturday 14th August was the worst day of the 1960s for me in spite of the 25 cops on the journey home from Winchester and being hauled by Merchant Navy Class No. 35023

Western Class diesel No. D1031 Western Rifleman approaches Exeter St David's station with a train for Paddington on 31/7/65.

Holland-Afrika Line. I had been going out with Pauline, my first serious girlfriend for eight months, but because our family holidays had not coincided I had not seen her for five weeks when I sped through New Brighton on my bike, that evening. In the interim, her Dad had decided that she was no longer to be allowed to see me.

I was not offered any explanation, other than it was thought our relationship might "get too serious". I was devastated. There are psychological observations amongst Freud and his followers, which offer explanations for a liking for train travel. For me, on occasions like this one, railway locations simply offered escapism from harsh reality. In fact, of course, it was really more of a place to go to feel sorry for yourself in an environment that you could be assured would not make matters worse and which might offer moments of respite.

I had always been a worrier, in fact I could have worried for England and all this meant my self-confidence took a nose dive. I wallowed in self-pity for ages. Over previous years I used to get the shakes, which I found was easily sorted out by eating something with sugar in it. I also used to get a sudden spaced out feeling, which always took me by surprise and made me panic.

This impacted on my train spotting activities, because more than once I turned down the opportunity to go on a long day trip with the school railway society, because I was fearful of getting one of these unexplained feelings then not being able to cope. I wanted to be close to home when they happened.

I got the sulks big time. I found an outlet and expression for my self-imposed isolation in music. That is what music does. You find something that suits your mood. I played the Walker Brothers' song, "Love Her", time and time again. It was a mournful ballad, full of regrets and missed opportunities.

I must have nearly worn out the grooves on the muffled organ introduction to The Animals, "Don't Bring Me Down". I read much later that they used an original hotel room, practice session take for this record, because they were unable to replicate that repetitive thudding backdrop in a studio. I found it totally haunting.

As was so often the case, trains also provided the antidote. So I went to Birkenhead sheds on 22/9/65 and copped Thompson B1 Class No. 61024 Addax and to Chester on 23/10/65, where, inexplicably, because I no longer have the proof in the form of a black and white image, my note book suggests I at least attempted to photograph Class A4 No. 60007 Sir Nigel Gresley, presumably on a special train.

Battle of Britain Class No. 34059 Sir Archibald Sinclair stands at the head of an express to London Waterloo at Bournemouth Central station on 3/8/65.

Unrebuilt Battle of Britain Class No. 34076 41 Squadron gets the right away from Bournemouth Central station with an express for London Waterloo on 3/8/65.

On the evening of 8/12/65 Ian and I went to the Zowie One event in the New Brighton Tower Ballroom. This was the first time we had been to a proper pop concert, other than with local bands at church halls or at school. I spoke to Tony Blackburn, who was then a DJ on the pirate Radio Caroline station and we were entertained by Paul and Barry Ryan, Twinkle, the Honeycombs, Brian Poole and the Tremeloes and the Yardbirds.

We reached Bournemouth on a family day trip by coach on 3/8/65, where I snapped West Country Class No. 34009 Lyme Regis in the centre road at the Central station, while the others no doubt went down to the beach.

This increasing fascination with the musical scene meant that when I finally graduated from reading comics to the New Musical Express. Along with the Melody Maker, it provided notice of new record releases, accounts of recent concerts and adverts for up and coming events. However, it would still be at least a year before we were going over the water to Liverpool for this reason, as well as for the trains and ships.

There was just time before the end of the year, for us to make another visit to Shrewsbury on 28/12/65. Britannia Class No. 70000 Britannia was on the sheds and I saw Manor Class No. 7820 Dinmore Manor for the first time. Most sheds now had scrap lines where condemned steam engines were parked prior to disposal and Dinmore Manor was one of seven of the class out of commission on that day in the county town of Shropshire [not Salop!].

Just in case there was any doubt about it, I took a shot of West Country Class No. 34009 Lyme Regis's nameplate as well [Bournemouth Central, 3/8/65]. Southern Pacific nameplates were very attractive, with the extra add ons of badges and scrolls.

Entering Bournemouth Central station from Waterloo rather too quickly for my camera is West Country Class No. 34034 Honiton, already minus at least one nameplate on 3/8/65.

Waiting for the off with a London bound express at Bournemouth Central on 3/8/65 is Battle of Britain Class No. 34060 25 Squadron.

Another express arrives at Bournemouth Central from the capital on 3/8/65, this time headed by Merchant Navy Class No. 35011 General Steam Navigation.

My parents dropped my sister and me off in Winchester for a week, after our Somerset holiday. My uncle was Head of Classics at Winchester College and we stayed in a house belonging to the school at Witham Close, in Kingsgate Street, right opposite one of the school gates. My uncle repeatedly asked me where I would like to go while we were staying with him and he seemed very perplexed when I told him day after day that Winchester station, by myself, would do just fine. I agreed to accompany him to Porchester Castle for a bit of culture on one day only, but I know that he never quite got it! I parked myself on a wall at the north end of the down platform at Winchester station, hour after hour and day after day. Battle of Britain Class No. 34090 Sir Eustace Missenden, Southern Railway paused with a Waterloo bound train on 11/8/65.

Looking north from the platform end at Winchester station on 11/8/65, during a brief stop for Merchant Navy Class No. 35011 General Steam Navigation.

Named Standard Class 5 No. 73111 King Uther approaches Winchester station with a passenger train heading towards Southampton on 11/8/65.

Unrebuilt West Country Class No. 34015 Exmouth approaches Winchester station at speed from the north on 11/8/65.

Unrebuilt West Country Class No. 34038 Lynton leaves Winchester station with a London bound train on 11/8/65.

Another view of West Country Class No. 34038 Lynton, pulling away from Winchester station on 11/8/65.

Battle of Britain Class No. 34087 145 Squadron is pegged to depart from Winchester station bound for London on 11/8/65.

Standard Class 4 No. 76069 pulls out of the loop, just north of Winchester station, on 12/8/65, with a parcels train.

Unrebuilt West Country Class No. 34019 Bideford draws into Winchester station with a southbound passenger train on 12/8/65.

Stanier Class 5 No. 44709 being turned manually on the turntable at Shrewsbury sheds on 28/12/65.

Looking rather forlorn amongst a line of withdrawn locomotives on Shrewsbury sheds on 28/12/65 was Manor Class No. 7820 Dinmore Manor, without its nameplates.

Also out of service is Ivatt Class 2 No. 46508, with its chimney wrapped up, on Shrewsbury sheds, 28/12/65.

Standard Class 5 No. 73090 and Stanier Class 5 No. 44966 stand at the entrance to the Shrewsbury shed buildings on 28/12/65.

Standard Class 4 No. 75006 looking grubby but still working, surrounded by other Standard and Stanier types on Shrewsbury sheds on 28/12/65.

Stanier Class 8F No. 48471 rests on Shrewsbury shed on 28/12/65.

First in the sequence of the Standard Class 5s, No. 73000 lies in store in a siding on Shrewsbury sheds on 28/12/65.

Regular train spotting companion Ian, ahead of a typical array of steam locomotives on one of our frequent Sunday cycle rides to Birkenhead sheds. The air was heavy with smoke, dust and the smell of sulphur, the ground littered with oil splashes, puddles of black water and potential pitfalls, literally, for those who were not always looking where they were going, but we did not care at all. We felt very much at home there. This undated photo could have been on any one of a number of visits, round about 1965.

A Stanier Class 5, this time the 2-6-0 version, No.42964, simmers in front of the gas holder at the side of Birkenhead sheds in this undated shot. I'm plumping for 1965 for this one.

A Hughes " Crab" Class 5 No. 42846 has an unrecorded Stanier Class 8F for company in this shot of the entrance to the covered shed at Birkenhead Mollington Street depot, round about 1965.

Another example of the Hughes "Crab" Class No. 42816 is attached to a brake van on Birkenhead sheds in 1965.

Chapter 6
1966

Britannia Pacifics were plentiful at Crewe on 3/1/66, but the only other named steam engine seen that day was Jubilee Class No. 45554 Ontario. The older ex LMS 4-6-2s had disappeared by then. The Brits had started to turn up at Birkenhead sheds too. No. 70020 Mercury was there on 16/1/66.

This photo of Ivatt Class 2 No. 43113 was taken adjacent to Crewe South sheds after another successful bunking mission, on 3/1/66.

At half-term in February Brian and I headed off to Newcastle. We stayed with Brian's older brother, in his student digs in Jesmond Dene. We went to see the Animals, performing on a revolving stage in a dance hall in their home city and they remain, to this day, one of my favourite bands.

Brian and I trawled round most of the Tyneside sheds and saw a lot of elderly ex LNER freight engines for the first time, many of them no longer in steam. Back at Central station towards the end of the day, I noticed a carriage on a southbound train had been reserved for Stoke City F.C. I don't think they would put up with anything less than a luxury air conditioned coach, from door to door, these days.

On the way back from Newcastle and already suffering from a nasty bout of the 'flu, I made a visit with Brian to Leeds Holbeck sheds on 28/2/66. This produced four Jubilees, Nos.

45574 India [yet again], 45597 Barbados, 45660 Rooke and 45643 Rodney. None of these were new to me, the only steam cops being Ivatt Class 2 No. 43070 and Fowler Class 4 tank No. 42161.

We knew these ex LMS Class 3F 0-6-0 tank engines as "Coffee Pots" or, more usually, "Jinties". No. 47450 is next to Crewe station on 3/1/66.

Aintree and the Grand National came around again. Only two named steam engines were evident this time, Britannia Class Nos. 70031 Byron and 70025 Western Star. By April and our next sojourn to Carlisle, it seemed like the border city was collecting up the whole class of them, with one in the station, six on Upperby sheds and a further twelve on Kingmoor.

The general election held on 31/3/66 was the first that I remember staying up for to watch the results coming in deep into the night, taking sides as if I was watching football or the boat race. My uncle had gone to Oxford University, so that is who we supported each year, in the annual televised event. Dad had rowed at school but I had no connection with it at all.

First in the series of the Hughes "Crabs" No. 42700, approaches Crewe station from the Chester direction, on a parcels train on 3/1/66.

I don't quite understand why this firm affiliation was so important to me, whether it was politics, football, cricket [the Priestleys were originally a Yorkshire family and the county had a good cricket team in the sixties], rowing etc, but it was. We were rooting for Harold Wilson to win, which he managed, with the help of Robert MacKenzie and his swingometer. I remember following affairs in Vietnam and the efforts of the American peace movement and the continuing permanent unease associated with the Cold War. I suspected that the "gozzy ghost cave" would not have saved us in the event of a nuclear catastrophe.

Massive demolition and rebuilding programmes were already visibly changing the 1960s urban landscape in Britain. Unfortunately from my perspective, as it turned out, this also included railway infrastructure. Inconsistently, I guess I was a conservative when it came to the railway scene and a radical elsewhere. Later on, whilst at college, I found out that

This was my first ever visit to the north east of England. My friend Brian and I planned a series of shed visits without permits, which turned out to be quite successful. Worsdell Class J27 No. 65789 was still in steam on North Blythe shed on 26/2/66.

this meant I was likely to be suffering from cognitive dissonance, in other words my views just did not add up and should have left me with an uncomfortable feeling in my head, as a result. This interpretation, my friends might be tempted to say, coincides with what they have been telling me for years!

I used to argue, rather stridently, my parents' corner, quoting stuff I'd overheard on the radio or read in the Guardian, which they had delivered to the house daily. Andy's parents were staunch Conservative supporters and my guess is that his dad saw me coming and rather entertained himself on my half-baked assertions.

Nevertheless there was definitely a prevalent tendency around in the suburbs to blame all the country's ills on the "bloody miners", "the bloody car workers" or the "bloody dockers", which was just about as categorically dismissive as my own, no doubt strident, utterances. Organised labour was seen as a real threat to the comforts enjoyed by the middle class.

Brian is just visible to the rear of Peppercorn Class K1 No. 62002. I think his arm waving is to indicate that this engine is not going to leave North Blythe sheds in a hurry, on 26/2/66.

My parents' politics could be summarised as benevolent paternalism, emanating from strong non-conformist, Christian family influences. My grandfather had been a Unitarian minister. Their beliefs were all about helping others and they voted with their consciences, rather than in their own self-interest. They knew that Labour victories could mean their having to pay higher taxes. They believed it was the right thing to do in order to promote a fairer society.

An unfortunate coincidence for railway enthusiasts living in Wallasey was that our Conservative MP was Ernest Marples, who was Minister of Transport at the time that Dr Beeching was appointed. Mr Marples, as he was then, was not massively into railways, as I recall. I remember seeing him canvassing at Seacombe Ferry, welcoming commuters returning home off the Liverpool boat with a loudhailer. Dad was one of his intended targets, no doubt, but I'm pleased to say he never gained his vote.

Andy has let it slip since that his mother was actually Mr Marples' secretary in Wallasey for a time, whilst John reminds me of photographs of him opening new motorway sections constructed by Marples Ridgeway, so he was not likely to be the most pro-rail of transport ministers, to put it mildly.

I still much preferred trains to politics. If Carlisle was collecting up the Brits, then Birkenhead sheds was doing its best with the Standard 9F 2-10-0s. There were twenty four members of the class present on 3/4/66.

Also on North Blythe sheds on 26/2/66 is Peppercorn Class K1 No. 62024.

Sometime in the spring of 1966 I made my second visit to Caergwrle by train. The reason for my vagueness about the date was that this was the first time I remember being embarrassed about being a train spotter, so I did not take my note book or record any numbers I had committed to memory. I went with a school friend Jim and two girls, Hilary and Vicky. Jim was not into trains but he was on a mission to befriend Hilary and I was toying with the idea of going out with Vicky on a more regular basis. We took a picnic, walked up to the castle in a repeat of my previous visit and I probably didn't even mention trains all day.

Minus its tender, connecting rods and front bogies on North Blythe sheds on 26/2/66 is Thompson B1 Class No. 61385.

For the first time I had felt a little self-conscious about my hobby. Should I be growing out of this? I suppose I felt under a little pressure to conform to the norms that I thought might be expected of me, especially in the company of those with no expressed interest. Some of my former spotting friends were showing little interest as well by then, though my immediate friendship group were still, literally, on board.

North Blythe sheds on 26/2/66 had a line of apparently withdrawn Raven Class Q6 locomotives, including No. 63389.

Conforming to the expectations of others was not a good enough reason to pack it in then and I'm pleased to say my rebellious streak still remains today. Self-confidence grows over time and I am probably as proud to be a railway enthusiast today as I ever was, even in the face of occasional ridicule. In fact, I'm certainly much more up front about it than I was as a young man.

On 14/5/66 Everton won the F.A. Cup, beating Sheffield Wednesday at Wembley Stadium, by three goals to two, having been 2-1 down. It was certainly going to be a memorable summer for football.

Towards the end of the decade we went to Goodison Park as a group whenever we could afford it and whenever we were not playing team football ourselves. In reality this meant it was often to evening matches. We chose the terraces known as the Paddock, which was opposite the tunnel from which the players emerged, indeed we could see them coming before the rest of the ground and therefore effectively started the cheering.

We were low down but close to the action and certainly within abusing distance of opposition wingers. A few youngsters somehow managed to get wooden boxes through the turnstiles and they parked themselves next to their dads and against the wall at the front of the enclosure, within sniffing distance of the turf.

Moving on to South Blythe sheds, we found Worsdell Class J27 No. 65812 apparently still operable [26/2/66].

When old men in the crowd collapsed or young kids needed rescuing from the crush and both seemed to happen alarmingly frequently, they were passed overhead to the narrow grass area alongside the touchline, before being stretchered away by volunteers from the St John Ambulance.

Unless you manoeuvred yourself right in front of the bars that were designed to prevent too much crush and movement amongst the crowd, you were literally swept off your feet and down the steps as part of a human wave, when the action on the pitch became concentrated in the least visible corner.

Sister engine, Worsdell Class J27 No. 65855 pulling a brake van past South Blythe sheds on 26/2/66.

However carefully you planned where to stand and however early you took your place before kick off, you could guarantee that at five minutes before the start a group of six foot blokes would wander in from the pub and squeeze right in front of you.

As we tip toed around sideways on our step, angling for a better view, our discomfort was immediately dispelled by the playing over the tannoy system of the drum roll at the start of the Z Cars theme tune, heralding the arrival of our heroes. It makes my tummy drop and the hairs stand up on my arm to this day.

The day after the cup final we celebrated by going back on the trains and found ourselves back with the Brits. At least they were still moving, as other classes were grinding to a halt. Britannia Class Nos. 70010 Owen Glendower and 70013 Oliver Cromwell put in appearances at Chester General station on 15/5/66, but I failed to record any signs of ex GWR steam there that day, for the first time ever. Consequently, we took a trip to Wrexham on 27/5/66 to try and locate some and we managed to find a handful of panier tanks on Croes Newydd sheds, though they were not in steam.

On 4/6/66 Ian and I went back to Manchester for a day at the cricket. We travelled by train, but the only new engine I saw all day was a Class 3F tank, No. 47493. The cricket was a bit more explosive, the highlight being a belligerent knock of ninety four by Colin Milburn, as England went down to the West Indies within three days.

Another view of Worsdell Class J27 No, 65855 from South Blythe sheds on 26/2/66.

I had reached the dizzy heights of the school second eleven, supposedly as a batsman. I think I scored a massive thirty six in one innings. I actually enjoyed fielding in the covers just as much, because I was potentially in the game for every ball that was bowled.

Come to think of it I was probably not far short in the field of some of the more substantially framed first class cricketers of the day. I liked to think I was a bit nippy over a short distance, as long as it was only ten or fifteen yards. We got a day off school for away matches, which I enjoyed hugely, with a free nosh too at some nice venues, like Rydal School in Colwyn Bay.

Raven Class Q6 No. 63445 at the buffer stops, in front of the round house at Sunderland sheds on 27/2/66.

I must have decided I was too old to go on holiday with my parents any more. After exams at the end of June, Ian and I set off for France, travelling by train, of course, but failing to record for posterity the train numbers on the other side of the English Channel. Our first wake up call on the continent was paying the bill in francs for sausage and chips in Boulogne. When we finally worked it out it came to fourteen shillings and sixpence each. It was a harsh lesson, learnt the hard way.

I remember clearly that we were steam hauled as far as Amiens, where an electric took over to take us to Paris. We saw the sights, staying in tents at the youth hostel at Suresnes. We retraced our steps as far as Etaples and took the cross country route towards Arras as far as Montreuil-sur-Mer, which is actually no longer on the sea. This 141R Class hauled journey, through charming countryside and in bright, late afternoon light, still provides pleasant memories. More dramatic to watch were the steam hauled Paris to Calais expresses thundering round the curve at the junction station at Etaples.

This holiday was also, I have to admit, noteworthy as the only time I resorted to minor vandalism for my entertainment. I unscrewed a sign from a train compartment, which read "Ne pas se pencher au dehors", which is the French equivalent of our, "Do not stick your head out of the window", or, more literally, "don't lean outside". I kept the sign for years, not displayed, but hidden in the same bedroom drawer that I used to amass bangers in the run up to bonfire night. It was representative of my darker side, obviously. In the end and possibly through guilt, I threw it away. It would probably make a few bob at auction these days.

On 30/7/66 England won the World Cup and within weeks, one of the heroes of the hour, Alan Ball, had signed for Everton from Blackpool. We had been playing football in the park and as we arrived back outside my family home, my Dad came down the path to tell us the news about our record new signing. We were delighted and our excitement was to be fully justified. Over the next few years, we regularly watched the midfield trio of Ball, Harvey and Kendall control game after game at Goodison Park, in the most stylish of fashions, their efforts culminating in the securing of the first division championship in 1970.

Another Raven Class Q6 No. 63458 at Sunderland sheds on 27/2/66.

We almost certainly went to the pub for a drink to celebrate both events. Pubs never figured highly in my mental list of desirable places. I didn't like the taste of beer, but it was already much more important for some of my friends, who, in the time honoured fashion, had got started on it well before they turned eighteen.

Having tried a series of pubs in the hope that they had a liberal interpretation of the licensing laws, my friends settled on the Nags Head in Rake Lane, which became our local and where they consumed large quantities of brown over bitter, while I kept them company with lemonade. The flat beer they poured out of large tins called Party Sevens, which they periodically dragged along to various gatherings was even less likely to swing it for me.

Peppercorn Class K1 No. 62007 stands outside Sunderland sheds on 27/2/66.

In the mean time, I celebrated the World Cup win by continuing my quest for independence. I went fruit picking, during the summer holidays, in the Vale of Evesham. I managed to see five Hymek Type 3 diesels whilst I was there, before I decided that I could live without Victoria plums, camp beds and no hot water and I made a hasty retreat to home comforts, after only one week away.

Birkenhead sheds was reliably still full of steam engines when we visited there on 20/8/66, with no fewer than twenty four Standard Class 9Fs, yet again. With nine more of the class on Edge Hill sheds and a further nine on Speke Junction on the same day, the area had become a stronghold for the big freight engines. Of course, they were still relatively young machines.

Worsdell Class J27 No. 65831 at Sunderland sheds on 27/2/66.

However, the pace at which withdrawals of the named steam locomotive classes that we had so prized was very apparent on that day. On all three sheds together we only saw three named engines, Stanier Class 5 No. 45156 Ayrshire Yeomanry and two Britannia Class examples Nos. 70014 Iron Duke and 70015 Apollo.

Alongside the withdrawals came the further proliferation of diesel types. It looks, from perusing my notes, as if I went to Chester the next day with the express intention of taking some pictures of steam to record its imminent passing. Before long, Chester too would be a steam free zone.

I did not see one new engine that day, but I photographed seven individual steam examples. It does not sound like a lot, but photography was always quite expensive; paying out for film and the developing charges, especially when a good proportion of the results were often wasted by poor decision making, lack of care and tricks of the light. I also had to weigh up

Displaying an open smoke box door at Sunderland sheds on 27/2/66 is Raven Class Q6 No. 63384.

camera costs against travel opportunities and throughout the period, actually getting there was usually the priority.

By the time I returned to Crewe on 26/8/66 I was copping more diesels and electrics than steam there too, in spite of a walk round Crewe South sheds, which was still full of them, including five Britannias. I photographed No. 70022 Tornado from the class because she was still in steam.

As if the regular inhalation of the sulphurous haze that emanated from steam sheds most of the time was not enough, we were also smoking more cigarettes. Most young people did, if our group was typical. We tended towards Embassy and Player's No.6. Ian and I had each brought large packs of two hundred Peter Stuyvesant and Royale, respectively, back with us from France.

The French themselves had been smoking Galois and Gitanes and eating a lot of garlic, usually just prior to using the Metro. I found these prevailing odours in Paris intoxicating. The whiffs from the drains and the flimsy "part see-through" public toilets in the streets added to the mix. What a shame they got rid of their dinky little, green, single-decker buses by the time we got back there again with our family. "Vive la difference"; but naturally France has changed too, in the interim.

We smoked because we thought we looked cool, though as I was not in employment throughout the period, I "cadged" [persuaded my friends to share theirs with me] more than I ever bought. Today none of us smoke, which has been, without doubt, a wise move for us all.

A tour of some of the Lancashire sheds by car on 11/9/66 unearthed plenty of surviving steam loco's and I saw nine that were new to me that day, as they were brought into the North West of England steam stronghold from other parts of the system, for the remaining couple of years of their existence.

On Crewe Works on 18/9/66 there were some diverse and noteworthy occupants including, ex Liverpool and Manchester Railway's "Lion", two Class A4s, Nos. 60010 Dominion of Canada and 60007 Sir Nigel Gresley, three ex Manchester to Sheffield Class EM1 electrics Nos. 26037, 26017 and 26055 and Class EM2 No. 27005 Minerva, presumably prior to scrapping. After the closure of Crewe North sheds, remaining steam was concentrated on Crewe South, which was still busy on that day.

Periodically, events occurred which struck home as being of major significance. The dramatic and untimely deaths of President Kennedy in 1963 and of the civil rights leader Martin Luther King in 1968 were high on that list, of course, but nothing affected me as much as Aberfan.

A quintet of Worsdell J27s occupy adjacent roads in Sunderland sheds round house on 27/2/66. The engines are No's. 65835, 65832, 65853, 65817 and 65788.

The disaster, which engulfed the primary school in coal slurry with such dire consequences, happened on the 21st of October 1966. We watched the forlorn rescue attempts on television. I wanted to go there and dig but was persuaded that it was just not feasible. It was the sheer hopelessness I felt and the fact that most of the victims were so young that seemed so unfair. Prompted by such events, it gradually dawned that life is often not fair in that very indiscriminate way.

We finished the year off in an unusual way. Spurning the excitement and obvious advantages of comfortable, warm, family Christmases, we decided to go to London. Ian, Dave, Grah and I set off to London on Christmas Eve, a day that most people were on their way home.

I have noticed, in giving my train spotting books the most careful scrutiny they have enjoyed for forty years, that they contain little side line gems that aid unexpectedly, yet massively, in prompting my memory. My summer holiday 1964 book told me that if I got into a pickle on my own, God only knows where in the West Country, I could phone the farm we were staying at, from a public, coin operated phone box, on Oakhill 395. What a comfort!

At West Hartlepool sheds on 27/2/66 is Peppercorn Class K1 No. 62004.

As far as our Christmas trip to London was concerned in 1966, I am very reliably informed by Ian and Grah, that we hitch-hiked all the way there, in two groups of two and met up in London. It was the first time we had tried long distance hitching.

Ian reminds me that when we were standing on the East Lancashire Road very early in the morning a police car pulled up and gave us a bit of an interrogation, to make sure we were not the recently escaped prisoners from Walton Gaol.

We somehow reached the outskirts of Birmingham. Our next lift is verified by the next surprise entry on the inside of the back cover of my note book.

Khan Asfer,
9, Hickman Road,
Sparkbrook,
Birmingham 11.

I believe that we met Khan at Gailey roundabout and that he kindly agreed to take us to London with him down an extremely empty M1 motorway. Somewhere near Luton his car conked out and could not be restarted. We abandoned ship and got to the capital with someone else, who was less forthcoming with their name and address. That afternoon, we paid at the gate to see Chelsea lose 2-1 to Liverpool. A strange thing to do, in retrospect, as all four of us supported Everton. Ian even went as far as buying a red and white hat to blend in with the Liverpool supporters, but his plan back-fired when he was threatened by some local hard knocks on the way out of the ground.

We failed to give Khan's generosity or his car's misfortune another moment's thought. We tried hitch-hiking once more on our way to the Lake District, but Dave's new lorry driver friend wanted him to join him for an impromptu "lunch" in a quarry, somewhere near Kendal and that kind of put us off any further involvement for a time.

To say that we found the capital less than welcoming on this occasion would be to seriously understate the situation. We took our photos outside the front door of 10, Downing Street, as you could in those days, we visited the main sights and then it gradually dawned on us that we were simply tramping up and down streets that the rest of the world had vacated for the Christmas holiday.

Return to Aintree and Stanier Class 5 No.45069 gets the home signal peg to approach the station, on a wet and overcast Grand National Day, 26/3/66.

The shops were closed, cafes too and we could certainly not afford the expensive restaurants that might have remained open. The Christmas Day penny dropped. We had nowhere to go for Christmas dinner.

Grah rang his uncle and aunt, who lived out of the centre in the Cricklewood direction. These were people he had hardly ever met. He explained our predicament and we were invited to join them. It felt to me like we had gate-crashed their family celebrations, much in the same way as we sometimes tried to wheedle our way into parties back home, that we knew were on, but where we had not been asked to join in. Dave insists their two daughters were really pleased to see us. They were all remarkably hospitable, given that at two hours notice there was double the demand for lunch.

Just visible through the mist is Britannia Class No. 70025 Western Star at Aintree station with a Grand National special train on 26/3/66. Anglo won the race that year, which I had forgotten, although I may have watched it on telly when I got home. On reflection, the snowy picture on our black and white telly was no longer a novelty by then, so I might have given the Grand National a miss.

What a strange set up, but how grateful we were to have been rescued from the streets in this way. By Boxing Day, with normality restored, it was off to Nine Elms sheds, for the twilight of Southern steam. The five new cops for me were all Standard tanks, but it was reassuring to see Battle of Britain Class No. 34089 602 Squadron, in steam and preparing for duty.

In a sign of the times, that would be repeated, I could not persuade my friends to come to Stratford sheds that afternoon, "just to see diesels" and they went off to watch Arsenal beat Southampton 2-0 instead, so I went round Old Oak Common as well. That would teach them!

Looking back, it could well have been a seminal moment, not in our friendship, but in our feelings about our hobby. I was never as excited about diesels and electrics as I was about steam. I carried on spotting them, because, increasingly, that's what there was to spot. Perhaps I still needed the connection with railways more than them. Perhaps they simply grew out of what some people no doubt regarded as a hobby that was for kids. In any event, I sometimes felt quite lonely about the whole thing over the next couple of years. Luckily, I could still persuade my friends to go out looking for steam rather than just going train spotting as such.

My recollection is that Britannia Class No. 70012 John of Gaunt has come off Kingmoor sheds and is making its way down to Carlisle Citadel station on 20/4/66.

Standard 9F No. 92080 is seen hauling a northbound freight past Carlisle Upperby sheds on 20/4/66.

From the road over bridge that led to Carlisle Youth Hostel, Stanier Class 5 No. 45185 is spotted backing down towards Kingmoor sheds on 20/4/66.

At the same location, Stanier 8F No. 48224 accelerates a short freight of covered wagons towards Scotland on 20/4/66.

Royal Scot Class No. 46115 Scots Guardsman contemplates a future in the public eye, at Carlisle Kingmoor sheds on 20/4/66.

Britannia Class No. 70037 rubs noses with a diesel fitted with snow plough in Carlisle Kingmoor sheds on 20/4/66.

Britannia Class No. 70016 has lost its nameplates by the time this photo was taken on 20/4/66 at Carlisle Kingmoor sheds.

Standard Class 4 No. 75048 takes water at Croes Newydd sheds at Wrexham on 27/5/66.

5700 Class panier tank at Croes Newydd sheds on 27/5/66

5700 Class panier tank No.9610 was in the round house at Croes Newydd sheds, alongside a Standard tank, on 27/5/66.

Our first venture abroad and to meet us at Boulogne for our train to Paris is 231K Class No. 231K37, part of a double header combination on 27/6/66.

French rail staff exchange pleasantries as 141R Class No. 141R1264 awaits the "right away", [what ever that is in French, Allez, perhaps] on 27/6/66.

141R Class locomotive, unconfirmed but likely to be No. 141R1264, moves its train away from Boulogne station on 27/6/66.

Our double headed express for Paris pauses at Calais Ville station on 27/6/66. The train engine is 231K Class No. 231K37.

The bay platforms at the north west end of Chester General station formerly served the Western Region lines, primarily the main line to Shrewsbury and Paddington and so through trains to Birkenhead reversed here. By 1966 this traffic was severely depleted. Stanier Class 4 tank engine No. 42616 stands at the head of a parcels train on 21/8/66.

A pair of Stanier 8Fs wait for duties in the centre road at Chester General station, led by No. 48074 on 21/8/66.

Stanier Class 8F No. 48548 pulls forward at the north west end of Chester General station on 21/8/66.

Stanier Class 8F No. 48548 eases its freight train past the water column at the north west end of Chester General station on 21/8/66.

Stanier Class 8F No. 48697 waits for the signals before backing off towards Chester sheds on 21/8/66. This picture was taken from the footbridge at the south east end of Chester General station, as members of the public take their lives in their hands on the crossing linking the platform ends.

Having taken on some water, "Jinty" Class 3F tank No. 47507 waits for some shunting action in the bay at the south east end of Chester General station on 21/8/66.

Stanier Class 5 No. 45282 calls at Chester General station with a passenger train for the North Wales line on 21/8/66.

Stanier Class 5 No. 44963 is all fired up and ready to go at Chester General station on 21/8/66.

Activity [and some inactivity] evident, as Britannia Class No. 70022 Tornado stands alongside the coaling stage at Crewe South depot on 26/8/66.

Two Stanier Class 5s at the south end of Chester General station as a DMU approaches on 26/8/66. Nearest to the camera is No. 45208.

Standard Class 5 No. 73136 is involved in some shunting, when snapped through the steel infrastructure of Chester General station on 26/8/66.

1600 Class No. 1628 busies itself on the centre road at Chester General station on 26/8/66, probably the last time I saw an ex GWR engine there in normal traffic.

On our way back to Birkenhead by DMU we passed Stanier Class 4 tank No. 42613, Chester bound, near Upton-by-Chester on 26/8/66.

Birkenhead Docks had a comprehensive railway layout fed by a branch which tunnelled under the town from the main line to Chester and then ran alongside the East Float dock. This shot of Stanier Class 8F No. 48266 was taken near to the point where the road to Wallasey crosses Duke Street Bridge on 23/12/66.

Stanier Class 8F No. 48266 passes the Royal Duke pub, on Duke Street, Birkenhead on 23/12/66. I remember seeing brand new British built diesels, sitting at the dockside next to Duke Street Bridge, waiting for shipment to Nigeria and other African countries.

Fellow enthusiasts Brian and Andy pose with me in front of one of Birkenhead sheds' Standard Class 9Fs, during a brief pipe smoking affectation in about 1966. [Photo Ian Hughes]

Crosti boilered Standard Class 9F No. 92023 on Birkenhead shed, some time around 23/12/66.

The John Summers iron ore trains from Bidston Dock to Shotton Steelworks were hauled by Standard Class 9Fs. No. 92047 is ready for duty round about the same time, 23/12/66.

Ian took this picture of Crosti boilered Standard 9F 2-10-0 No 92023 on Birkenhead Sheds. My estimation is that the date was 16/1/66.

Probably taken on the same day, 16/1/66, I am posing in the cab of Class 3F tank No. 47495, out of steam on Birkenhead sheds. [Photo Ian Hughes]

On our strangely timed visit to London for Christmas 1966, we trekked around Nine Elms sheds on a cold and crisp Boxing Day. Battle of Britain Class No. 34089 602 Squadron is in steam and receiving attention as the shed yard brazier glows brightly, 26/12/66.

A close up of Battle of Britain Class No. 34089 602 Squadron's nameplate at Nine Elms sheds on 26/12/66.

Standard Class 4 tank No. 80143 at rest on Nine Elms sheds on 26/12/66.

Merchant Navy Class No. 35027 Port Line at Nine Elms sheds, 26/12/66.

Nameplate and badge of West Country Class No. 34004 Yeovil, in need of a little TLC, on Nine Elms sheds, 26/12/66.

West Country Class No. 34004 Yeovil is partially lit by a watery sun at Nine Elms sheds on 26/12/66.

Merchant Navy Class No. 35029 Ellerman Lines at Nine Elms sheds on 26/12/66, oblivious of a future with its innards laid bare to the world at the NRM.

Standard Class 5 No. 73086 on Nine Elms sheds, 26/12/66.

Standard Class 4 tank No. 80140 catches a bit of low winter sunlight in Nine Elms sheds on 26/12/66.

My friends had abandoned me to go and watch a first division football match so I went out to Stratford sheds by myself. Numerically, first in the class of the English Electric Type 3 diesels, No. D6700 is looking well tended on 26/12/66.

Chapter 7
1967

Psychedelia, in 1967 and indeed afterwards, rather passed me by. I was offered pills and weed at parties and declined. I have always been a little on the cautious side. Instead of hanging out, dropping out and all the rest of it, I carried on having a groovy and cool time train spotting.

Hughes "Crab" Class 5 No. 42942 is a rather forlorn sight at the side of Birkenhead sheds on 3/3/67.

I started the year with a visit to Birkenhead sheds on 3/1/67 and met Standard Class 9F No. 92073 for the first time, but that was the only new one, out of the forty three steamers on shed. Chester sheds had a similar complement on 12/2/67, as did Crewe South on the same day. Crewe Works entertained three Class A4s, with the addition of 60026 Miles Beevor to the two we had seen on our last visit, as well as Standard 9F Class No.92220 Evening Star.

We went back to Chester on 4/3/67 to see two Castle Class specials arrive from the Shrewsbury direction, optimistically going first to photograph them as they approached the city at speed near Saltney, which was not a particularly good move from a photographic point of view, but it was nevertheless a nice sight to behold.

On a dismal day, weather wise, 24/3/67, I tried to photograph the Britannia Class locomotives on Carlisle Kingmoor sheds, but the results were disappointing. There were a lot of steam engines present, but I think many were withdrawn. On our way to Whitby by coach on a sixth form field trip with the geography department on 3/4/67, we called in at York and in my allotted couple of hours free time there I went to the sheds to find Class that A4 No. 60019 Bittern was the only Pacific around.

I can't remember ever taking a portable radio with us when we went train spotting. The two things just didn't go together. In June 1967, a large group from our local church youth club went for a walk on the tow path of the Shropshire Union Canal near Upton-by-Chester. This involved our setting off on the No. 10 bus again to Woodside, then transferring to a green Crosville service, the company which served much of South Wirral.

On 4/3/67, the second half of the "two Castle feast" of special trains is provided by Castle Class No. 4079 Pendennis Castle approaching Chester at speed near Saltney. I was obviously in two minds about attempting a panning shot.

I was with my new girlfriend Chris, later to be my wife and she brought with her, though I seem to remember I carried most of the way, a fairly substantial portable radio. "A Whiter Shade of Pale", by Procol Harum, was played so frequently that we adopted it for ever as our song. The diversion she had caused was such that I did not note a single train number on that day.

How important was music at every stage. There is something matched up, etched in the memory for every critical instance. Some of the sounds were so sparklingly novel and the introductory few bars so breathtakingly beautiful and fresh. They maintain their attraction however much I hear them. Firmly in this category are:

Moody Blues	"Go Now"
The Kinks	"Waterloo Sunset"

Beach Boys	"California Girls"
The Who	"Pinball Wizard"
Pink Floyd	"See Emily Play"

I first met Chris outside the Derby Bathing Pool. She was on her way home late one afternoon in the spring of 1967 to start her paper round in Wallasey Village. We were playing football on the sands at Wallasey Foreshore, thus completing our gradual migration towards the sea for our footballing venues. This one could be adversely affected by the wind, which, at the drop of a hat, would whisk the ball off towards Wales. I was very taken straight away with her permanent smile and her obvious joie de vivre. I was quite impressed with her rather daring mini dress too.

Castle Class No. 7029 Clun Castle arrives at Chester General station with "The Zulu" special train on 4/3/67.

In order to maintain the balance in my life I headed to Birkenhead sheds on 21/6/67 with my camera. By now it was a matter of recording steam's passing when we could and we were aware that there was not long to go. There were thirty eight examples on shed, dominated, as had become usual, by Standard Class 9Fs and with just a handful of diesels present.

In addition to taking photos I bought some sound recordings of steam trains in action. They were mostly vinyl EPs [extended play] of the original recordings made by Peter Handford and marketed on the Transacord label. The exception was a Ffestiniog Railway example, which made a clumsy attempt to simulate the typical conversations that might be over heard in the station booking office or on board the train in the refreshment car.

We rolled about laughing at these staged and stilted efforts.
Customer, in a posh voice- "Two and two halves to Tan-y-Bwlch, please"
Booking office clerk- "Two and two halves to Tan-y-Bwlch, sir?"
To which, we added- "Yes, Two and two halves……." And so it went on, with us ad- libbing interminably. I guess you just had to be there.

Castle Class No. 7029 Clun Castle receives suitable admiration from those on the platform on 4/3/67.

There was also a detailed transaction recorded in the buffet car, in which some drinks were being ordered when a shrill voice pipes up in the background, "I'd love a cup of coffee". It joined the lexicon of much mimicked phrases that acted as unofficial passwords for our friendship group. Only we knew what we were talking about half the time. Young people continue to create their own part languages, of course. It helps with the bonding process and creates little exclusion zones, some no-go areas for over inquisitive adults.

I feel proud to have retained a bit of "scouse" about the way I speak, though my Mum said I had no trace of it until I went to work in Birkenhead. My middle class parents were certainly without it. Proper Liverpudlians would describe all of us Wirralians as "plastic scousers" anyway.

I like the way accent and coined phrases add to the notion of regional identity and therefore to a sense of belonging, for example in my affinity to the Evertonian tribe. Our park and platform speak in the sixties might also have had a bit of spiky, youthful rebelliousness about it. Our most overused terms included:

> "All right, Ace" – a typical greeting to a friend.
> "Bagging off" or "Tapping off" – making a new female acquaintance.
> "Spied it" – felt sudden shame or embarrassment.
> [Yer] "Jokin!" – are you sure? I don't believe you.
> "All me arse" – not very good.

For our summer holiday in 1967 Ian, Grah and I went to Devon, by train, staying for a week in youth hostels and starting at Bath on 22/7/67. Three days later at Salcombe youth hostel I received a letter from Chris. The reason I know this is that she did what I considered then to be an extremely girlie thing and kept all our correspondence thereafter.

A view of the cab side of Castle Class No. 7029 Clun Castle in Chester General station on 4/3/67.

Initially the letters came thick and fast, though I have to admit they tailed off some what over the next few decades. I am suddenly very grateful to her for hanging onto them. Her holiday messages in the summer of '67 were all about the difficulties of tuning in to Radio Caroline in New Milton [hardly surprising given the two ships' locations in the Irish Sea and the Thames Estuary], having to rub shoulders with the crowds of hippies on the beach and the "long and boring" [?] train journey from Birmingham to Southampton, which was relieved only by the fact that she was able to buy shandy on board in the buffet car.

I obviously still had some work to do in persuading her of the important contribution trains can make to our quality of life. John suggests that this scenario could be a suitable subject for a Glen Baxter drawing and having checked him out I can see what he means. In any event, it was a long job but worthwhile in the end.

Even for us seasoned enthusiasts the holiday itself was now firmly the focal point, rather than the trains. We saw Class A4 No. 60026 Miles Beevor again at Crewe on the way down south. Though I was recording and copping lots of diesels, I did not see one steam engine that was new to me, all the time we were away.

I must have dispensed with my anorak years before and upgraded to a cagoule for inclement weather. This, however, was the "Summer of Love" and I remember raiding my Mum's wardrobe for suitable items to wear for youth club. I toyed with, but eventually turned down, all her beads and bangles, in favour of a bright red cardigan to put over my blue and white hooped tea shirt. How cool was that?

I don't think the dress code for going round sheds had changed a lot by 24/9/67, when, at Crewe, I saw a number of Stanier Class 8Fs I had not seen before, and two more at

Birkenhead sheds on 15/10/67. It was quite a relief to cop something that wasn't an 8F, when I saw Stanier Class 5 No. 44877 for the first time at Speke Junction sheds on 12/11/67.

We carried on up by car to Spring's Branch sheds at Wigan that day and one of our number stole a lamp from a bracket on a disused piece of rolling stock. I am told that the guilt is with him to this day, though the lamp may not be. We were a little disillusioned by now, to see such communal disregard of the whole infrastructure and I guess we just fell into the trap of apathetic resignation. I copped 39 that day.

Castle Class No. 7029 Clun Castle's name plate shines in the sunlight at Chester General station on 4/3/67.

By the end of 1967 a lot of railway installations had a ghost town feel to them. Even the sheds which had been earmarked to keep steam going in the North West of England had an unreal and decaying air about them. Most had long lines of withdrawn engines. Many of those still working were clearly not in good mechanical order, leaking steam from a variety of orifices and having an unkempt and uncared for appearance. There was no need to ask permission to enter the sheds any more or adopt a strategy for bunking them. No one was bothered whether we were there or not.

Wigan Springs Branch, Wrexham Croes Newydd, Carnforth, Walton Junction and Lostock Hall all came into the ghost town category, eventually. It was possible to go round sheds and not see a single railway employee during your visit. It took a bit of the edge of the event, really. No adrenalin rush response to taking a risk, just lines of dirty engines that nobody appeared to be interested in apart from us.

By now there was so much else to do and so many demands on limited finances. Empowered by our attendance at Zowie 1, 1967 was the year we started to attend pop concerts in earnest. We saw Jimi Hendrix, Pink Floyd, The Move, Amen Corner, The Nice, The Who, The Flowerpot Men, Arthur Brown, Traffic and others during the latter half of the year.

I increasingly aligned myself with bands that we described as being progressive rock, ones that were trying new things and not simply out for a sing-a-long top ten hit single. The Nice, Pink Floyd, Vanilla Fudge and Yes [from 1968] came into this category. The pleasure of sharing the experience of live music from my favourite bands stays with me to this day.

I got round to seeing almost everyone I wanted to see performing in concert, with the exception of the Beatles. We came close with Vanilla Fudge. They dropped out of a tour we had tickets for before they got to Liverpool and my wife and I heard Cactus, which contained some of their personnel, from outside the venue, which was lakeside in Montreux, Switzerland in the 1970s and even then quite by chance.

Castle Class No. 7029 Clun Castle, sporting "The Zulu" head boards, recovers from her exertions at Chester sheds on 4/3/67.

I had begun my last year at school in 1967. Our new building at Leasowe had only been open for a few months. On Monday 6th November I happened to glance outside from a first floor window, during a sixth form private study session, to see a plume of smoke, a newly painted red buffer beam and the unmistakable outline of a Standard 9F rounding the curve out of Bidston station, a couple of miles away across the Moss. I put two and two together straight away. It had to be the last steam hauled John Summers iron ore train.

Another view of Castle class No. 4079 Pendennis Castle, resting on Chester sheds on 4/3/67.

Consequently, we went to Birkenhead sheds for the umpteenth time on 3/12/67, to investigate. They were all gone. My notebook says I copped two diesels. It is the last page in my note book. I did not go there again. An era had come to an end. It has struck me since that at times like that it is a really good idea to have multiple interests, so that if things go wrong in one area, for example a heavy Everton defeat, then solace can be gained by moving swiftly to another activity. In political terms, I remember the alternative, rather myopic view of the world, being referred to as "single issue fanaticism", by the commentator Bernard Levin.

By now the BBC had begun broadcasting in colour. Soon afterwards, our friend Tony, who had never been a train spotter but who had a back garden big enough to play cricket in, became the first of our group by a mile to have a colour telly. It was massive, encased in a hefty wooden cabinet. We were invited round to watch Football Focus on Saturday lunch times. The colours concerned were green [the pitch and the players] and red, which wrapped itself around the footballers like a hooded track suit, in a way reminiscent of a later advertisement for a warming breakfast cereal.

On the last two days of 1967 I returned to Barry with my friends, Ian, Grah and John. We were driven down by Andy, in his parents' white Hillman Minx, No. LHF 819. How trusting they were, though admittedly Andy had a reputation for being a very sensible chap, compared to the rest of us. He reminds me that we actually had a rather hairy journey over the snow covered Brecon Beacons and also encountering practical precautions on the roads, involving disinfectant and straw baths for tyres, to counteract an early foot and mouth scare.

On the way, we called in at Cashmore's scrap yard in Newport to view the assembled Southern Pacifics waiting to be scrapped there and we did not reach Barry until after dark on 30/12/67. We stayed in a bed and breakfast opposite the site, which was close to the docks. When we drew back the curtains in the morning on New Year's Eve the bulging sidings were in full view. It was, I remember, a cold, bright and windy day, interrupted by heavy showers. This time I took some pictures to help me remember some of the locomotive types I had seen previously, under happier circumstances.

Castle Class No. 4079 Pendennis Castle's footplate crew take centre stage on Chester sheds, 4/3/67.

We thought we would never see these particular engines again. Instead, of course, they just keep on adding to our enjoyment, as we rediscover them still, on the plethora of privately owned heritage railways that have grown up in the interim. Indeed, it's worth stressing that without the Barry haul, many of the private lines probably would not exist in their present form.

I was still recording all my cops in my Ian Allan Summer 1962 Combined Volume, priced at eleven shillings and sixpence, often referred to by other spotters as "combines". I formerly had a "locoshed" book, which I operated simultaneously as a safeguard, in case any thing happened to my "com vol", as we preferred to call them. I never took the combined volume out of the house. Locoshed books listed all locomotives in rather small print in a pocket-sized hand book and showed the home shed code of each one. I left mine on a train when I got off at Chester and the value of a back up system was proved beyond all doubt.

I possessed various other combined volumes from time to time. I also had Aidan Fuller's Shed Directory, which was invaluable when, for example, planning a shed bash round Birmingham. There were, in addition, separate Ian Allan books for the different regions' locomotives, somewhat complicated by the arrival of the Standard classes, I suppose.

I was interested to read a Guardian colour supplement interview in October 2009, in which Michael Palin described his 1955 Combined Volume as his most treasured possession, so I'm in good company, as far as that is concerned. With a liking for railways in general, that is two things that Michael Palin and I have in common. My wife is quick to remind me that that is where any comparison ends.

Castle Class No. 4079 Pendennis Castle takes a break on Chester sheds, having arrived in the city on a special train on 4/3/67.

Standard Class 5 No. 73035 pulls away from Chester General station on 4/3/67 with a passenger train bound for the North Wales coast.

Crosti boilered Standard Class 9F No. 92026 prepares for action, at the end of the station platform at Chester General on 4/3/67

Crosti boilered Standard Class 9F No. 92026 perfectly placed for a photo, behind brazier, water column and signal at Chester General station on 4/3/67.

Crosti boilered Standard Class 9F No. 92026 making its presence felt, whilst leaving the south end of Chester General station on 4/3/67.

Crosti boilered Standard Class 9F No. 92026 gets its train away from Chester General station in the direction of Crewe, on 4/3/67.

(Above) Stanier Class 4 tank No. 42613 with specially painted buffers has arrived from Birkenhead in the covered former "Great Western" section of Chester General station, on 4/3/67.

(Left) Stanier Class 4 tank No. 42613 simmers near the buffer stops in the bay platform at the Hoole Road end of Chester General station on 4/3/67.

Britannia Class No. 70006 Robert Burns in store at Carlisle Kingmoor sheds on 24/3/67.

Smoke box door gaping and without nameplates, Britannia Class No. 70008 Black Prince is out of service on Carlisle Kingmoor sheds on 24/3/67.

Britannia Class No. 70027 Rising Star stands at Carlisle Kingmoor sheds on 24/3/67. The steam appears to be emanating from a locomotive on the other side of the Brit.

Britannia Class No. 70052 Firth of Tay at Carlisle Kingmoor sheds on 24/3/67.

The replacement painted on nameplate of Britannia Class No. 70040 Clive of India was not untypical in the final days of steam, at Carlisle Kingmoor sheds on 24/3/67.

Britannia Class No. 70010 Owen Glendower on Carlisle Kingmoor sheds, 24/3/67.

Britannia Class No. 70002 Geoffrey Chaucer on Carlisle Kingmoor sheds, 24/3/67.

Britannia Class No. 70022 Tornado passes below the road bridge, south of Carlisle Kingmoor depot, on 25/3/67.

Standard Class 9F No. 92135 makes her way to Carlisle Kingmoor sheds on 25/3/67.

Britannia Class No. 70051 Firth of Forth was photographed on Carlisle Upperby sheds on 25/3/67.

Andy alongside Britannia Class No. 70051 Firth of Forth on Carlisle Upperby sheds, 25/3/67.

Britannia Class No. 70029 Shooting Star pokes out from Upperby sheds in Carlisle on 25/3/67.

Ian in the company of Britannia Class No. 70012 John of Gaunt on 25/3/67 at Carlisle Upperby sheds.

Ivatt Class 2 tank No.41264 lying neglected at Carlisle Upperby sheds on 25/3/67.

Ivatt Class 2 No. 46522 on Carlisle Upperby sheds, 25/3/67.

Ivatt Class 2 tank No. 41217 at Carlisle Upperby sheds, on 25/3/67.

Stanier Class 4 tank No. 42663 stands overlooked at the back of Birkenhead sheds on 21/6/67.

Standard class 8F No. 48450 is one of a number of engines in steam in the yard at Birkenhead sheds on 21/6/67.

Standard Class 9F No. 92100 on Birkenhead sheds on 21/6/67.

Stanier Class 4 tank No. 42613 with a class mate, adjacent to the coaling stage at Birkenhead sheds on 21/6/67.

Stanier Class 4 tanks 42613 and 42647 at Birkenhead sheds on 21/6/67.

Standard Class 9F No. 92218 hauls it's load of John Summers' iron ore hoppers away from Bidston Moss on 2/8/67.

Standard Class 9F No. 92218 with a full load of imported iron ore bound for Shotton Steel Works from Bidston East Dock, near Woodchurch, in mid Wirral on 2/8/67.

Stanier Class 5 No. 45130 is seen operating tender first on a short permanent way train near Woodchurch on 2/8/67.

No smiles, just inquisitive looks from the footplate crew of Stanier Class No. 45130 as she pauses near Woodchurch on 2/8/67.

Standard Class 9F No. 92163 makes her way cautiously across Duke Street in Birkenhead. Road traffic was delayed by flashing lights and on some occasions by policemen on point duty, as shown here [2/8/67].

Standard Class 9F No. 92163 moves slowly past the Blue Funnel Line transit sheds on 2/8/67. There are examples of three different vintage transport types visible in this one shot.

Britannia Class No. 70045 Lord Rowallan is ready for the off at Crewe station on 24/9/67, alongside Bo-Bo electric No. E3022.

Standard Class 9F No. 92086 on a still busy Birkenhead sheds, 15/10/67.

Here are some of the moving parts belonging to Standard Class No. 92086 at Birkenhead sheds on 15/10/67.

A broadside view of Standard Class 9F No. 92113 on Birkenhead sheds, 15/10/67.

Pistons and some other critically important bits of Standard Class No. 92113 on Birkenhead sheds, 15/10/67.

Our return to south Wales on 30/12/67 took us firstly to Cashmore's scrap yard in Newport. Here we saw West Country Class No. 34047 Callington.

Standard Class 3 tank No. 82031 awaits dismantling in Cashmore's Newport scrap yard on 30/12/67.

West Country Class No. 34104 Bere Alston is waiting to be dismantled on the scrap line at Cashmore's of Newport on 30/12/67.

West Country Class No. 34008 Padstow receives a visitor at Cashmore's scrap yard in Newport on 30/12/67.

Modified Hall Class No. 7927 Willington Hall has finally reached the buffers at Barry on 31/12/67.

2800 Class No. 3862 languishes at Barry scrap yard on 31/12/67.

A rooftop view of King Class No. 6023 King Edward II, at Barry on 31/12/67.

Modified Hall No. 7927 Willington Hall and others, at Barry on 31/12/67.

An aerial view of Manor Class No. 7822 Foxcote Manor, at Barry on 31/12/67.

5101 Class No. 4156 picks up the sunlight on 31/12/67 at Barry.

5101 Class No. 4110 in the long grass at Barry on 31/12/67.

Battle of Britain Class No. 34059 Sir Archibald Sinclair with very white smoke box door hinges at Barry on 31/12/67.

Standard Class 4 No. 75079 at Barry on 31/12/67.

A broadside of Battle of Britain Class 34059 Sir Archibald Sinclair, at Barry on 31/12/67.

West Country Class No. 34101 Hartland stripped of its nameplates and its dignity at Barry on 31/12/67.

Merchant Navy Class No. 35022 Holland-America Line at Barry on 31/12/67.

Standard Class 5 No. 73082 Camelot at the buffer stops at Barry on 31/12/67.

Rain glistened "spam can" casing can't disguise the sorry state of unrebuilt Battle of Britain Class No. 34072 257 Squadron at Barry on 31/12/67.

Modified Hall No. 7927 Willington Hall in bright winter sunlight on 31/12/67, at Barry.

Rusty smoke box door of Battle of Britain Class No. 34070 Manston at Barry on 31/12/67.

5700 Class No. 9682 in the company of other ex GWR engines at Barry on 31/12/67.

5700 Class No. 3738 looking the worse for wear at Barry on 31/12/67.

The air smoothed casing of Battle of Britain Class No. 34070 Manston at Barry on 31/12/67.

A view of the obsolete chimney of Manor Class No. 7822 Foxcote Manor at Barry on 31/12/67

5700 Class no. 4612 boasts a splash or two of white paint at Barry on 31/12/67.

Chapter 8
1968

This is where things start to get a bit more difficult. My spotting note books end in December 1967, yet I have an overall record of where I went and how many new cops I entered in my Ian Allan books, thereafter. I must have lost a book at some stage, or else I had just have written on scraps of paper, until I formally recorded the results, on a day to day basis.

In any event, Ian and I went back to Newcastle on 23/2/68 and I have to say the visit was more memorable for reasons other than trains. We stayed with Ian's sister in her student digs and as Brian and I had done on our previous visit, we went to see a live band in the evening. It was the Jeff Beck Group. We knew of Jeff from his days with the Yardbirds. We had acquired their autographs when they had played at the New Brighton Tower Ballroom. Jeff had with him a promising youngster, who played the mouth organ. So we got to see Rod Stewart, at no extra cost. We watched Newcastle United beat Wolverhampton Wanderers 2-0 at St James's Park on the Saturday afternoon. I think we saw a lot of diesels over the weekend as well.

Heading for Preston, near Ormskirk, is Stanier Class 5 No.45411 on 16/3/68.

After that, we revisited some old haunts, including Carlisle in March, where I copped thirty five new engines over the two days. This visit was marred by a minor car crash in the middle of Carlisle. Dave had been allowed by his parents to drive John, Ian and myself up to Carlisle Youth Hostel in their smart, two tone Ford Cortina No. CHF 516 D.

In steam on Carnforth sheds on 16/3/68 is Stanier Class 5 No. 44897.

Suffice it to say that when Dave crossed the red traffic light, although his attention was clearly not where it should have been, we were certainly not doing anything to aid his concentration. In his defence, he reminds me that a combination of "a wet reflective road surface and additional females on board" had added to his problems. I'm not sure if these would count as mitigating circumstances, if the affair had had more serious consequences. Luckily, no one was hurt, but it put the dampers on our fun temporarily, at least until the necessary repairs had been made.

As 1968 wore on I had to give more serious thought as to what I was going to do when I left school. I was not in the frame for university and the annual careers convention gave precedence to banking, insurance, shipping companies and the armed forces, none of which appealed to me and that was about it. Not surprisingly, I fancied working on the railways, so I applied to start a management course and was granted an interview in Euston House, Eversholt Street, London on 17/4/68.

Britannia Class No. 70021 Morning Star is pictured amongst a line of withdrawn engines at Carnforth sheds on 16/3/68.

This meant looking unusually smart for a day, but more attractively, an early morning full English breakfast on the Liverpool Lime Street to London Euston express, free of charge, a delight I have never repeated since that day. I passed the interview and entry to the training programme was to be conditional on my passing my "A" levels. It was a great day out. I copped forty locomotives as well.

Standard Class 4 No. 75015 is withdrawn from service on Carnforth sheds, 16/3/68.

Thus encouraged by copping diesels, it was off to Manchester with another five additions on 7/6/68, this time with Ian to Old Trafford, for day one of the England versus Australia test match. The proceedings did not loom large in my consciousness for long, though I believe we saw batting from Geoffrey Boycott again, partnered this time by John Edrich.

I finally left school in July 1968, having stayed an extra year to top up my "O" levels before being allowed to start advanced studies. There had been just too much going on to give school work the attention it required. I was a bit exasperated with the old grammar school ethos by the time I finished.

Throughout the 1960s I felt that people often treated us a little differently because we were "grammar gogs". To some extent they still can do and it is built on an assumption that you automatically received a superior education, which in some ways was probably the case, but that was not the whole story.

In contrast to being stimulated by some inspirational teaching from some bright and comparatively adventurous younger members of staff, I also spent an inestimable numbers of largely wasted hours laboriously copying factual material from a blackboard. The Sunday school prize winning italic writing that I had taken up to senior school with me lasted no more than the first few minutes of the initial orally dictated note taking session. It never recovered from the shock. There was just no way you could hope to re-fill an Osmiroid fountain pen with Quink Royal Blue ink, without missing at least two sentences.

A discarded Standard Class 4 No. 75021 exchanges the time of day with a VW Beetle on 16/3/68 at Carnforth sheds.

More importantly, the bi-partite system seemed to me to perpetuate what appeared to be fairly deep social divisions. I questioned a lot of the prevalent values and attitudes they tried to instil.

"You are the cream of Wallasey", the woodwork teacher had yelled at us some years before, just prior to throwing, in disgust, my nearly completed and only slightly flawed wooden tea pot stand, with its carefully bevelled edges, to the far end of the room. Supposed superiority and complete humiliation all in one go. That was about par for the course.

My rebellious streak was fuelled by two incidents that happened whilst I was in the sixth form. Firstly, I was sent home for having long hair and told not to return until it was no longer touching my collar. I railed at that, though I felt very sixties and progressive as well, but I conformed after a good moan. An added complication was that my Dad was chairman of the school old boys' association at the time and I did not want to put him in an embarrassing situation.

Standard Class 4 No. 75024 is out of use at Carnforth sheds on 16/3/68.

Secondly, I was smacked on the back of the head by an elderly history teacher, who had seen me talking during private study in the library. I was nineteen and I felt humiliated, hurt and angry. He apologised to me a couple of days later.

In the company of a class mate, Standard Class 9F No. 92004 is part of a siding full of withdrawn locomotives at Carnforth sheds on 16/3/68.

Though I had been caned three times at junior school, I never received it at the grammar. Though the cane was available and used sparingly, teachers there often took the law into their own hands, literally, whether it was wielding a gym shoe or a wooden board duster. Such random acts of violence by teachers were still relatively commonplace when I started my own teaching career. Although thankfully this is no longer the case, unfortunately teachers themselves can be on the receiving end quite a lot these days, which of course, is just as wrong.

Ian and I headed back to the continent for our summer holiday. We organised a circular tour by rail, with ticketing arranged through Frames travel agents in Whitechapel, Liverpool. Starting from Calais we went to Lille, Brussels, Paris, Luxembourg, Bonn, Cologne, Rotterdam and then back via the Hook of Holland to Harwich. From memory, evidence of continental steam was confined to the Calais region on this round trip. We were primarily sight-seeing and exploring, staying in a string of youth hostels along the way and returning home on 3/8/68. We were back just in time.

Standard Class 9F No. 92077 is still in steam and moving about the yard at Carnforth sheds on 16/3/68.

On Sunday 11th August 1968 I walked down to New Brighton station with Ian, Grah and John and took the Mersey underground electric train to Liverpool Central, this being before the link to Lime Street station had been made. I try to imagine how we felt and largely, I fail.

Since early 1967 and probably before that, other aspects of our lives as friends growing up together had mushroomed. Girlfriends had become more important. We still played park football and cricket constantly and many of us were now members of teams, playing on Saturdays and even Sundays, times when previously, we might have gone looking for trains.

Standard Class 9F No. 92212 is sandwiched between two other withdrawn engines at Carnforth sheds on 16/3/68.

Through Grah's work we played in Liverpool on a Sunday morning for a time, as members of a team called Mersey Freight Conveyors and Stevedoring Football Club. We played competitive badminton in the week, in addition to regular Thursday club nights at Liscard Congregational Church, which we knew as the "Congs". This was a one court hall so matches often lasted until after midnight.

We amused ourselves off court by strumming our badminton rackets in imitation of Pete Townsend's extravagant guitar style. Home matches were quite civilised affairs, in which both teams would sit down and eat tea together half way through the evening, while Ian got to know Jenny a bit better, behind the stage curtain. It was whites only for these matches, except for the middle-aged ladies, who additionally wore beige tights. That must have got a bit sticky in the middle of summer.

Ian and I even went to church at the "Congs" and though our attendance was patchy, we dipped in a few times during the seven years covered here. We were persuaded to do so because we were excused the prospect of having to fidget our way through the tedious sermons.

Instead, Dave, a younger member of the congregation with a brief to look after the teenagers, took us out into the badminton hall, where we sat round on a circle of chairs and discussed the burning issues of the day, supposedly from a religious, or at least from a moral, standpoint. I found it stimulating and quite enjoyed being asked to sound off about things. I didn't usually require an invitation to give my two penny worth.

Some of us played table tennis for the Y.M.C.A. team as well, though this was the only reason I ever went there. As a result, I even played a representative table tennis match for Wallasey under 18s. I did not distinguish myself, while nonchalant Barry Drinkwater, normally a rival from the Moreton club, was almost certainly putting his opponents to the sword. It was just nice to have him on our side for a change. I was not asked again. School and college work had become more important for some, though I could not yet claim to be in this category.

On the 11th August 1968 Stanier Class 5 No. 45110 is ready to depart from Liverpool Lime Street for Manchester and Carlisle with the Fifteen Guinea Special, officially the last steam train on British Railways.

None of our other activities were much consolation when the day finally came. We walked into Lime Street station. It was chocker. We debated how best to get close to the action. Should it be platform six or platforms seven and eight? I think the train was in six, so we thought if we could get to the end of the longer seven, we might get a better view looking back.

The few policemen around already looked harassed and overwhelmed. They could not have been expecting such a large crowd. I tried to take a picture from a permanent ladder fixed to a signal. I was told to get down and my place was taken by someone else, straight away. I tried to manoeuvre my way back through the throng to the platform edge, to get an uninterrupted shot of Stanier class 5 No. 45110. I was shoved backwards into the crowd by another policeman, presumably because I was too close to the danger zone. I gave up and stood in the middle of the crowd. As the train left I tried to poke my camera between kids sitting on their Dads' shoulders and a lot of people who were taller than me, [which was most].
That was it.
In 2008 I summarised it in this poem.

The end of steam in sixty eight

August eleven was the date
for the end of steam in sixty eight,
an event destined to deflate,
but what a crowd on platform eight.

A "black five" turned out, not a crate,
with driver proud and fireman mate,
fire burning brightly in the grate,
days numbered, what would be her fate?

Whistle to lips, as cheeks inflate,
last train departs from this estate.
Thunderous echoes at last abate,
last whisps of smoke they could create.

Trudged sadly homewards through the gate,
we thought we had been born too late,
no cinders falling on your pate,
the country now a diesel state.

Although there was no one to hate,
I really couldn't get it straight.
It left me feeling quite irate,
steam, then, just pictures at the Tate.

But progress onward at a rate,
means now the situation's great,
a new "Tornado" to elate,
so all things come to those that wait.

To complete my misery, the next week I found out my "A" level grades were not good enough to take me into the railways as a career. I felt a bit aggrieved for a time, because a year previously I believed Bernie Yarnold had been admitted to the same management training scheme on what were reputed to be lower grades, but I may be doing him a disservice here. I wouldn't want to be thought of as holding yet another grudge for upwards of four decades.

Maybe I was lucky in the long run. I will never know for sure. I started teacher training that October, while I made up my mind about what I really wanted to do with my life. Forty two years later I'm still in education, but I've got an idea or two now about how I might like to spend my time.

Stanier Class 5 No. 45110 is waiting for departure from Lime Street Station Liverpool on 11/8/68.

Heads.

Bottoms.

Hands.

All Over.

John, Ian and Grah walking back to Liverpool Central Low Level after the events of 11/8/68.

Taking stock. Reflections on the train home with Ian, Grah and John. "What shall we do now then? [11/8/68]

Chapter 9
Since 1968

I carried on going spotting for a time, but I was often on my own. John reminds me that we went out looking for withdrawn steam engines on scrap lines at Crewe, Lostock Hall and Edge Hill. Strange as it seems, we returned to Lime Street in October 1968 to see Alan Pegler on the footplate of his preserved LNER Class A3, No. 4472 Flying Scotsman.

It was never as much fun again, because it had always been a group activity and consequently a very sociable experience. We were and still are great friends. We grew up together and we still frequently meet up. We had a fabulous time when we went train spotting. We never shut up. We entertained each other all day, winding each other up, making fun of each other and of the people we met, in what we described as "skitting". I wouldn't have missed it for the world.

I chose to explore the railway scene further for a time on a series of rail rover tickets, either on my own or as a way of seeing new parts of the country with Chris. When we got married and started a family, I advocated the South Devon Coast as ideal bucket and spade territory. My wife was not fooled, but we spent many happy summer weeks in Teignmouth and Dawlish, within view of the famous sea wall, before poor weather drove us to France. It wasn't Castles and Kings, but to start with at least, it was Western diesels, which I thought was about as good as they got.

When I stopped going spotting I still kept a note of things I saw incidentally, when sent on courses from work to London, for example, by writing the odd number on the corner of the Guardian newspaper. I kept in touch by buying the magazines, visiting the preserved lines and more recently, by following the resurgence of steam on the main line. As locomotive hauled trains have given way nationally to all sorts of units, enthusiasm has taken another dent.

In 2008 the National Railway Museum wanted to commemorate the fortieth anniversary of the end of steam on British Railways and in particular, the running of the Fifteen Guinea Special from Liverpool Lime Street, in August of that year. My friend John replied to their advert in the railway press and we were invited to join in the celebrations at York.

We met some of the retired enginemen, who had been employed on the day in 1968 and our own recollections were filmed for posterity by the NRM. We contributed to a series of Radio Five interviews, which were broadcast late one evening when every one had gone to bed, as part of a programme marking the event. I felt proud to be so closely associated with the movement, although our only contribution had been to go and say goodbye to No. 45110.

I was asked to write a piece, describing our reminiscences, for the museum's archive, where, it is already likely to be gathering dust, [or perhaps show cased as part of the recent Search Engine developments]. In it, I wrote that as a result of an early introduction to the railways, together with our school trips,

"the beauty, excitement, camaraderie and atmosphere of the steam railway was set alight in us........" and the events of 1968.........."would bring to an end an era that had really only recently begun [for us]...... Overall, I felt a bit cheated, because I was born just a few years too late to make full use of the glorious 1950s and early 1960s steam era. For us it was to be all over on this day and we were still teenagers......... We trooped back home, a disconsolate bunch. We have made the most of it since, of course, preservation and all that and the magnificent return of express steam to the main line. I'm still proud to have been a train spotter. It is the magic of steam. Either you feel it or you don't."

I wrote the poem overleaf to help me bring back memories of the countless times I'd called into station buffets all over the country. The ones that stood out for me most were Chester, between the main entrance and the GWR bays and Exeter St David's, on the main down platform. I was particularly keen on a wide, flat chocolate biscuit that came in blue for milk and red for dark chocolate, the name of which escapes me still. A strong mug of tea was a good stand by on a cold day and I probably had a lot more sausage rolls than were good for me.

I liked going into cafes in every town I was in and I was well known for it, apparently. Andy said I would write a book about cafes one day and he may end up being right. All town centres had cafes but they were sometimes called milk bars or coffee bars. Milk bars sold coffee and coffee bars sold milk. They had other things in common. They had a small range of goods for sale by modern standards. They tended to smell of fried food and have ineffective air extraction systems, which led to the windows being permanently misted up.

Concessions to modernity included a single sign in the form of a flashing light and a juke box or games machine, but probably not both. The food served was basic and unimaginative. The layout was typified by cheap furniture and formica surfaces. Where there were older wooden tables they were covered in heavy but easily wiped oilskin table cloths.

The application of herbs and spices and the imaginative use of salad was a generation away. Food was not refrigerated or vacuum-packed and the sandwiches, hiding under a perspex cover, on occasions, really did curl up at the edges. The coffee, which was never "real" coffee, but always instant and often mixed with chicory [yuck], was spooned out of industrial sized tins. Come to think of it they really offered us little incentive to leave the confines of the station buffet and walk into town.

Mike Pryce

This was the iconic photograph taken on Sunday, August 11, 1968, when the last steam train chugged out of Lime Street Station, Liverpool, and into railway history – or so everyone thought. It appeared in the following day's national newspapers and in countless magazines since.
John Beck, above, wearing a white shirt, managed to elbow his way to the front of the thousands of steam enthusiasts.

We really believed it was the end of the steam train

Forty years ago thousands of trainspotters gathered in Liverpool to witness the end of an era. Malvern lecturer John Beck was among them

IT was one of those occasions when no one knew quite what to do. In the end, no one did anything and 40 years ago the final journey of the last mainline steam train in Britain began in total silence.

About two thousand spectators had crammed into Lime Street station, Liverpool, on the morning of Sunday, August 11, 1968, to witness what they believed would be the death of the golden age of the railways. But as Stanier class locomotive 45110 slowly pulled away from the platform, belching smoke and hissing steam, not one person raised a cheer or shed a tear. Not out loud anyway.

Then, suddenly, the air was filled with the sound of two thousand cameras clicking and whirring to capture the historic scene for posterity. As if in reply, the locomotive let out a long, eerie shrieking whistle that echoed around the station's cavernous roof like the last scream of a dying animal.

Right in the middle on the front row, in about as prime position as the elbowing crowds would allow, was young John Beck. His face was centre stage in the iconic image of the day, which dominated news coverage of the event and later appeared on book covers and in railway magazines.

Today, John is head of art and design at the Chase College in Malvern, but back in 1968, he and three mates were among the crush at Lime Street.

Forty years on: From left, Graham Sullivan, Ian Hughes, John Beck and Michael Priestley together again after that eventful and emotional day in 1968.

He recalled: "The one great memory of the day is the silence that fell over the whole platform – in fact the entire station – as the train inched forward and then reluctantly began its farewell. The hush seemed unreal, even surreal and the feeling right through my bones that something significant was happening will always stay with me.

"It was as if nobody knew quite what to do. Eventually, after what seemed an eternity, the silence was broken by some tentative clapping."

The train got its name from the fact the 420 passengers on board had each paid 15 guineas to be part of history. For their money, they were taken on a 314-mile round trip from Liverpool to Manchester and Carlisle and back. On the way there was a cold lunch with champagne, high tea and other refreshments and everyone received a souvenir scroll and a ticket. John said: "How I wished I was one of the lucky people on board. I remember thinking it somehow seemed unbelievable there would be no more steam after that day. That's what we all thought then. The death of steam. That's what everyone was saying. The railyards were already full of locomotives waiting to be broken up. Little did we know there would be a new steam era with the emergence of the preservation scene."

John Beck was born in New Brighton on the Wirral, a short ferry across the Mersey from Liverpool and first became entranced by steam railways in the late 1950s, when his family travelled by train for summer holidays in the Lake District.

John became much more than just a train spotter and as a teenager travelled all over the country looking at railway sheds and other parts of the steam scene.

With the final steam journey taking place on his doorstep, it was a day not to be missed. The train was due to depart Lime Street station at 9.10 on the morning of August 11 and well before John rendezvoused with three friends Michael Priestley, Graham Sullivan and Ian Hughes.

He said: "We thought we would be nice and early, but we hadn't anticipated how many people would be there that morning. They were hugging the platforms and anywhere that would give a half decent view. The place was heaving.

"We made the considered decision of which platform to go for and then slowly went about moving along it to see how far we could get. Amazingly we made it virtually to the end, just before the platform edge sloped away. We stood there among the crowds, taking in the atmosphere of this very special occasion. Everyone seemed to have a camera. It was exciting, but sad at the same time because no one thought they would see steam again. This was, we thought, the end."

The locomotive chosen to pull the 10-coach train out of Lime Street was a "bread and butter" Stanier class no 45110, known as The Black 5. This hauled to Manchester Victoria where the bigger Britannia Pacific class Oliver Cromwell took over for the long stage to Carlisle via Blackburn and Ais Gill.

The Stanier took over again at Manchester on the return trip, but when it eventually rolled back into Lime Street at 19.50pm at the end of its historic journey, the platform was almost deserted.

"There was hardly anyone there to see it return," said John, "which looking back today probably seems strange. But we'd had all our excitement in the morning and the day was a bit flat by then."

FOOTNOTES TO A DAY IN HISTORY

There are two footnotes to this story.

First, by happy co-incidence, the Stanier class loco 45110 never went to the great scrapyard in the sky.

It was rescued, restored and is now one of the stars of the Severn Valley Railway, which runs between Kidderminster and Bridgnorth.

Second, John Beck's father worked in the centre of Liverpool in the early Sixties and every lunchtime used to walk past the entrance to the Cavern Club in Matthew Street.

John said: "From street level he could hear the Beatles playing down in the basement,"but he never went in."

Which was as bad, if not worse, than missing the last day of steam.

Liverpool, August 11, 1968. From left, John, Ian and Graham. Michael had the camera and took the picture.

The fortieth anniversary of the end of steam on BR was recognised by the Worcester News in an article in their 26/5/08 edition by Mike Pryce. Mike interviewed local resident John Beck about his reminiscences of seeing off the Fifteen Guinea Special from Liverpool Lime Street station on 11/8/68. I am grateful to the Worcester News for permission to publish this article.

Bought sandwiches were a massive disappointment in the 60s, compared to the variety available today; tasteless, thin sliced white bread, Webb lettuce and tomato, with cheese or ham, was about as exciting as it got. There is an impressive variety on offer these days by comparison, from a much wider range of fast-food outlets, or so I thought until I visited the United States. On the other hand, a colleague whose wife works in a sandwich factory tells me that he will not under any circumstances buy one pre-packed. He assures me he has good reason for wanting to see exactly what is going into it.

The Station Buffet

Swing open the door and peer into the cavernous hall,
dimly lit, high ceilinged, with dark wood surround,
floor tiled, diagonal black and white,
heavy tables, leather covered chairs abound.

Thick set mirrors, embossed with hard edged designs,
between the polished panels on the wall,
where posters show healthy, smiling families,
beach scenes from Devon and Cornwall.

Behind the glass, all kinds of tempting fare,
biscuits with forgotten names, cheese scone,
the massive, hissing urn in pride of place,
spits scalding water in the tea pot all alone.

The bustling overalled staff eager to please,
exchange their jokes then disappear out back,
whilst travellers trip over luggage, catch a nap,
check timetables, choose papers from the rack.

A rumble, then a roar, the building shakes, brakes squeal.
The late express grinds to a halt in platform four.
Staff shout, announcer urgently performs his task.
Green flag is waved, steam whistle blown, a last slammed door.

In my defence, it was one of my first efforts.

It's almost impossible to exaggerate how unfashionable train spotting has become in the years since the 60s. Even an interest in railways is often seen now as an anachronism, a throwback to a long-gone age.

There seems to be an unofficial hierarchy of acceptable hobbies, with doting on celebrities at the top and railways firmly at the bottom. It does not surprise me at all in this age of reality TV shows, where participants are encouraged to be as judgemental and nasty as they can be to each other, constantly hovering on the boundaries of the distasteful and the unacceptable, in the chase for ratings.

How we got there is subjected to a thorough investigation from the perspective of the cultural historian, by Ian Carter, in his book British Railway Enthusiasm. He draws attention to the psycho analysts and subsequent commentators who surmised at the links between train spotters and those diagnosed with Asperger's Syndrome or autism.

In the conclusion to her entertaining quest to identify the essential characteristics of the condition of being English from a sociological perspective, Kate Fox goes a step further. On page 401 of "Watching the English" she writes, "The English social dis-ease is a congenital disorder, bordering on a sub-clinical combination of autism and agoraphobia [the politically correct euphemism would be 'socially challenged']." So we have all got it. The predisposition to be train spotters who don't otherwise get out much lurks within all of us Anglos, including the scousers. Presumably it gets a bit watered down towards the Celtic fringe, though.

The loners who may eventually have hastened the negative stereotype and became the archetypal butt of the train spotter joke certainly existed. We used to meet them on the platform ends, next to the brazier and under the water column. The few who stood out as different weren't typical train spotters.

One got the impression these lads were never that far from home. Train spotting was a cheap hobby if you lived within cycling distance of a fairly productive stretch of main line and a lot of lads of limited means spent their formative years there, or on their local station. It could be very parochial. They might have classed their Semis but never have seen a King or a Streak.

A combination of child rearing and teaching experience suggests to me that over protective parenting can sometimes hinder a child's ability to make friends easily. Denying them the opportunities to experiment in the art of socialising with others from an early age might be damaging to their subsequent ability to relate positively to other children.

There may be nothing wrong with the child's cognitive processes but if a lack of engagement causes additional shyness or awkwardness it could lead to rejection or bullying by their peers, encouraging further withdrawal and so the problems may escalate. That might make it more difficult to discriminate between those with an innate predisposition for developmental disorders and those whose socialisation has simply gone wrong.

If the lonely lads we met on the platform required time out from their own harsher realities and they must have taken some stick at school and in their communities, why not get that solace on a station platform? Most of the spotters they met would have been positively benign, compared to the aggro they would no doubt have received from some of the baddies in their home environment. School children can be very cruel to each other.

Still at it after all this time. Former spotters and still close friends, Andy, Dave, Ian, John, Mike and Grah at Blackburn station enjoying one of the Cotton Mill Express specials, in the company of Stanier Class 5 No. 45407 The Lancashire Fusilier, in September 2008.

By chance [perhaps some people would suggest it's too much of a coincidence!], I have spent the last five years working closely with autistic youngsters. There are some emphatic common characteristics shared by most of the students I come into contact with, which would make their condition apparent to strangers within a minute or two of having first made their acquaintance.

I imagine that for their parents, diagnosis must come as a hammer blow. Having had three "neuro-typical" children, [the term the experts like to use, to contrast with those with Autistic Spectrum Disorder], I can only begin to contemplate their initial anguish and admire their eventual stoicism, as they galvanise themselves for the task that faces them for the rest of their lives.

Most of the parents I have met are so totally focused and positive and their offspring are so obviously loved and well cared for, in the face of significant challenges to the family unit. It is difficult to express this without sounding patronising but I often feel seriously humbled by them.

For the most part, these autistic youngsters are a delight to work with and support. A high proportion claim a liking for trains, perhaps the sorts of numbers on average that you might have expected across each cohort in the 50s, at the height of the train spotting craze. Some of them repeatedly watch Thomas the Tank Engine programmes on their computers, much in the same way as I read and re-read the Reverend W. Audry books, on which they are based, when I was a child.

An enthusiastic and talented colleague, whose perspective on the issue is one I'm inclined to take note of, points out the dangers of labelling the young people we deal with. She pulled me up when I felt tempted to suggest that autism traps these young men [and comparatively fewer young women] in their childhood.

The fact is that the maintenance of childhood interests into adulthood does not prevent autistic young people being happy. Some with Asperger's Syndrome acquire detailed knowledge and skill in different areas of experience and it is important to herald their achievements whilst continuing to support their social development.

Mike, Grah, Ian, Dave and Andy at Blaenau Ffestiniog for a trip to Portmadoc on a warm and sunny Saturday, 26/9/09. At the port we ate lunch in the pub and watched Everton beat Portsmouth on the television. It was the perfect day.

Some academics prefer to see autism as simply a different way of looking at the world. They avoid making value judgements about whether the perspective of those diagnosed is any better or worse than our supposedly normal one. Nevertheless, autism remains a disability for many, often denying them access to the enrichment that comes with continued education and the fulfilment that more complete cognitive development allows.

For the rest of us, maintaining an interest in trains into adulthood can be part of a rich and varied existence, in which all the other expected traits of maturity have, hopefully, if in some cases rather belatedly, fallen into place and where railways take their position alongside a number of other healthy activities and interests.

Train spotting leads to all sorts of other grown up hobbies within the railway sphere [the railway fancy, as Ian Carter calls it], whether its railway modelling, photography, transport history, "hands on" engineering, volunteering support for the private lines, collecting railwayana or membership of the countless clubs and associations connected with past and current railway enthusiasm.

Sad as it is, this is not likely to be how things pan out for young people with autism. In most cases I've seen, of young people between school age and twenty five, their life of dependency is only just beginning. They are never likely to make the developmental leap from childhood to adolescence, never mind to maturity. Thomas the Tank Engine and going to the swings could well end up being popular and reassuring mainstays for good, dependent on the sustained support required to access them.

The autistic guys I know who profess an interest in trains, don't do train spotting. With autism, in just about every case I've seen, come learning difficulties. Even train spotting can be a cognitive leap too far, requiring as it does some control of numeracy, including ordering and classification, as well as fairly acute powers of observation, some organisational skills and a reasonable dose of initiative.

There is some support for an overlap between higher functioning autism and Asperger's Syndrome, a supposedly related condition in which communication and conversation are not so restricted [in fact, sometimes quite the opposite], but where the accepted norms of social interaction are not followed. Those diagnosed tend to go into great detail about their specialist subject areas, without picking up on the signs of boredom setting in with their intended audience.

In my limited experience of observing Asperger's Syndrome close up, I have known a graduate mathematician with an amazing knowledge of past sporting moments and more than one young person with a fascination for computer games but railways has not figured amongst their obsessions, though I don't doubt it does for some. Intense interest in something is not sufficient reason to label people as suffering from this or any other disorder, though I suppose the way they relate their passion to others might be grounds for concern.

I remain a little perplexed about some of the diagnoses for Asperger's Syndrome and of those at the "higher functioning" end of the autistic spectrum, who don't seem to share the characteristics of the autistic majority. Its difficult to avoid thinking that there is a considerable group of people here that the experts are not sure what to do with, in the face of demands for help from bewildered parents, desperate to give a name to their children's problems, actual or perceived. In circumstances where educational support and access to the benefits system rely on a diagnosis being made, there could be added pressures to find one.

My hunch is that a lot of work remains to be done before there is any certainty about the accuracy of diagnosis and in establishing boundaries for these two conditions. It will be fascinating to discover how they eventually unravel the relationship with other manifestations, like obsessive compulsive disorder, attention deficit hyperactivity disorder, some aspects of mental health and the impact of social factors.

All of the above may not leave a lot of room, eventually, for eccentricity or marked personality differences. The Diagnostic and Statistical Manual of Mental Disorders lists alphabetically 410 conditions, including 5 Pervasive Development Disorders, which usually first become apparent during childhood. Autism and Asperger's Syndrome are two of these.

I felt driven to see what it also had to say about obsessions. How obsessive is collecting things, whether it's train numbers or artifacts? On pages 456 and 457, under the section entitled Obsessive Compulsive Disorder, it remarks that diagnosis demands "recurrent obsessions or compulsions that are severe enough to be time consuming [i.e. they take up more than 1 hour a day] or cause marked distress or significant impairment. At some time during the cause of the disorder, the person has recognised that the obsessions or compulsions are excessive or unreasonable."

I guess I'm still in the frame with the first section but I think the rest of it lets me off the hook. Whereas my wife may sometimes insist that my interests are obsessive, I can honestly say that this does not worry me at all. In fact, I love all my interests - bird watching, collecting railway posters and carriage prints, Everton F.C., playing badminton, going to the gym, writing as now until after midnight, watching steam trains etc. Any doubts in my mind have been caused by the aspersions cast by others and because I've felt under attack as a result of their comments.

Back on our more familiar lines, from being a participant in a fairly main stream activity for generally well adjusted young people, anyone admitting to an interest in trains today can become an object of ridicule. Unreasonably, the term train spotter itself has become an insult, meaning someone with an inadequate personality, in short, a misfit.

It has become shamefully acceptable to be negative, castigating and judgemental, about just one out of many hundreds of harmless pastimes, none of which have to suffer anything like the same level of invective as ours does. I have recently been told I am a geek for coming out over my interest, whilst some one else said that my liking for bird watching is, "better than trains, at least." So what's wrong with trains?

As Matthew Engel succinctly put it in his admirable book Eleven Minutes Late, it became, "a generic term of abuse for anyone seen as over-interested in any subject, instead of following the more acceptable national trait of languid apathy".[p.25]

Nicholas Whittaker, in his entertaining reminiscences entitled Platform Souls, pointed out that the scorn poured on train spotters is partly a consequence of a culture that has become obsessed with cars. He wrote, "Interest in any other form of transport is regarded as eccentric. Fast cars and posh cars are aspirational, but railways [and buses] are seen as a second-class form of travel, ergo any interest in them must be suspect and pitiable". [p.11/2]

Media driven stereotypes and labelling should be challenged with good humour. I don't feel a need to get too defensive or heavy about it. I think that my young mentor at work feels I am possibly over-reacting a bit. She says the colloquial use of the term "train spotter" today is merely cultural shorthand, rather than a thorough judgement. Perhaps I am just a bit too touchy about it.

My friend John pointed out that the prevalent anti-railway prejudice was interrupted more recently by the widespread publicity for and the general media interest in the new build Peppercorn Class A1 No. 60163 Tornado, when it was unveiled in 2008. He mentioned a quote he had come across from a spokesman of the A1 Trust, "For once you didn't have to defend your interest, but you had people coming up to you saying what you did was fantastic."

Everybody to their own thing is my maxim. It is surely the variety of available hobbies and the fascinating specialist and focused interests and the detailed research that often results, which add to the spice of life for everyone.

A gentleman I know who is now in his 70s, who regularly used to go to watch Gresley Pacifics passing through Grantham in the 1950s, told me recently that he had been into his local newsagents and found the pin up magazines at eye level and the railway press on the top shelf. I'm not even going to try to analyse that one.

I had occasion recently to visit an industrial estate in Birkenhead, in connection with another book I was having published. I looked up the location on the internet and discovered that it was adjacent to the former Mollington Street entrance to Birkenhead sheds.

On arrival, I parked my car and looked down onto the sizable, but still derelict, former railway site. I peered through the seriously robust railings and remembered us swinging into Mollington Street on our bikes on Sunday mornings forty five years ago, to the occasional look of disdain from the few residents about at that time. Their terraced houses have not survived either. Come to think of it the high rise flats that would have re-housed them could have gone by now as well.

We parked our bikes and knocked on the foreman's office door. We asked politely if we could look round. The foreman always looked us up and down and appeared to be making a judgement based on our appearance and demeanour. Perhaps he sussed we were grammar gogs and not scallies. He nodded assent without speaking, adding as we turned towards the entrance, "Make sure you let us know when you are finished". We did as we were told.

Where the long grass now waves in the wind, we had sought out the B1s and Granges, the odd Jub or Hall, amongst the familiar giant 9Fs. We inhaled the stale air as we systematically zig-zagged our way up the roads, to record the day's attendance. We climbed the gradual incline as far as the coaling stage and we checked we hadn't missed any thing down the sides of the sheds and next to the gas holder, which still stands. When we were done we stuck our heads round the door and said thanks and we spun off across the docks to our respective Sunday roast dinners. Mine was always lamb. I won't touch the stuff now.

After that it was straight down to Elleray Park for football. No time to digest your food. Pick the teams and it was the first to twenty. Dave and John's dad would shout to them to come for tea from over Auntie Flo's garden wall, with the score at seventeen all and we would all groan in unison and insist they stayed to the bitter end.

For the rest of us, a more leisurely stroll up to our house, with my tight bronze jeans split at the knee, Adidas Rom trainers soiled and smelling of grass stains and my thighs tightening up nicely. We were just in time for my Mum's chocolate cake with a cup of sweet tea. Shoes off at the door, we settled down to Alan Freeman's introduction to Pick of the Pops on the Light Programme, "Hi there, pop pickers".

I have still not quite finished with train spotting. At the time of writing, I have never seen Royal Scot Class No. 46100 Royal Scot. I am closing in on her and soon we will meet. She is quite a star performer to sign off with, after all. When I see her I will underline the number in red biro, in my Summer 1962 Ian Allan combined volume and then I will only need four "Scots" and that, of course, is how it will stay. I think that will probably be an end to it.

On the other hand, I just can't help myself noting the numbers of the Class 66s on the coal workings through Worksop, when we call in for a drink at the station café, with the students from the local college where I work. My eyes gravitate uncontrollably towards the number and the odd nameplate. I meant odd as in infrequent, but actually names like Peterborough Power Signalbox and Willesden Traincare Centre leave me cold.

There is usually a small knot of elderly gentlemen to be found on Worksop station. In inclement weather, I often interrupt them in the Railway Café, huddled round a table, drinking hot tea and exchanging views about the abandonment of the crew signing on point in Worksop yard, the latest garish colour scheme for the Class 66s or the seemingly rather circuitous routes taken by some of the freight workings in the area.

On the walls are framed handbills with British Railways totems, black and white photos from a different age of a whole galaxy of steam hauled Saturday holiday trains to Cleethorpes and Mablethorpe in the 50s and later special trains headed by "Sir Nigel" or "The Scotman", when calling at the station. A replica seatback sign, a three dimensional representation of the night train on The North East Route from London to Aberdeen in the nineteenth century, boasting "525 miles in 10 hours", with a tiny clock embedded in it that appears to keep good time, a crop of current railway magazines in a rack and a copy of a 40E Colwick shed plate provide further adornments.

In summer they hold their meetings on the platform and take photos of the coal trains rattling over the Carlton Road level crossing, hoping that some "jobs worth" railway employee won't pick them up over activities conducive to endangering national security. They are a recognisable and reassuring part of their community, helping passengers with accurate, if unofficial, travel advice, contributing to the coffers of the splendid station café and enjoying each other's company with stories from their own railway golden age. Good luck to them, in their consistent and continuing pursuit of their benign yet engrossing hobby.

When I had a few minutes to kill while my car was being serviced recently, I strolled down into Lowdham village in time to see the 9.36 two car DMU from Leicester to Cleethorpes pause at the station. Only two people got on but a mother with a small child in a push chair stayed on the platform and then it registered with me that they too had just stopped by to watch the train. The conductor/guard shouted to the mum "I'll give him a blast on the horn" and as it pulled out he did just that. It could have been me, but for the 60 year gulf of time that has elapsed. They want to watch that sort of thing. It can be habit forming.

On 7/11/09 Ian pointed out to me an article in the Guardian of that day which claimed, rightly in my view, how lucky our post war generation has been. Far from missing out, we have indeed enjoyed our own golden age. No further world wars, greater affluence, the revolution in popular music, the benefits of dramatic technological advances, relatively sound pension schemes, free and improving health care at the point of demand, global travel opportunities etc. You could add solutions to hitherto seemingly intractable problems, like the end of the Iron Curtain, the troubles in Northern Ireland and apartheid in South Africa.

On a more personal level we would probably want to add a World Cup and Everton's four championships. I didn't see all my Kings or A4s either, but I missed World War Two and 1950s National Service. In the words of the song, it is a case of "Reasons to be cheerful, one, two, three" and probably a lot more. I'm happy to settle for that.

My first inclination was to call this book Just in Time [for the end of steam in 1968] but then I thought that would be bit of a cop out. I was a train spotter. We were train spotters. It's a book about train spotting, so that is what it is. Train Spotters. Don't be mealy mouthed, just face the flak head on.

Dedication

This book is dedicated to my great friends and fellow former spotters,

Ian Hughes,
Andy Mace,
John Beck,
Dave Beck,
Graham Sullivan.

Ian's mum died today, Monday 3rd October 2011. She was nearly ninety. Our parents' generation has now passed on in its entirety. Their view of the world was characterised by a firm commitment to family life. They stayed together and they were always there for us when we needed them.

They forked out for our railway expeditions and listened to our tales of the day when we came home wearing a veneer of perspiration and coal smuts. They encouraged our friendships and our hobby. The days of coconut cake and heavily sweetened tea are long gone but our memories of the time are alive and well.

Bibliography

Ian Allan, The abc of British Railways Locomotives Combined Volume, Summer 1962, Ian Allan Ltd

American Psychiatric Association, Diagnostic and Statistical Manual of Mental Disorders, Fourth Edition, 2000, A.P.A., ISBN 978-0-89042-024-9

Ian Carter, British Railway Enthusiasm, 2008, Manchester University Press, ISBN 978-0-7190-6566-8

Matthew Engel, Eleven Minutes Late, 2009, Pan Books, ISBN 978-0330-51237-4

Kate Fox, Watching the English: The Hidden Rules of English Behaviour, 1975, Hodder and Stoughton, ISBN 978-034081862

Philip D. Hawkins Tracks on Canvas, The Railway Paintings of Philip D. Hawkins, 1998, The Oxford Publishing Company, ISBN 0-86093-538-8

Nicholas Whittaker, Platform Souls, 1995, Indigo, ISBN 0-575-40011-0

Christian Wolmar, Fire and Steam, 2007, Atlantic Books, ISBN 978-1-84354-630-6

The Guardian colour supplement, 7/11/09

The Liverpool Daily Post and Echo, 1963

The Worcester News, 26/5/08

Ian Dury and the Blockheads, Reasons to be Cheerful, The Best of Ian Dury and the Blockheads, Ian Dury, CD, 2005, Music Club Deluxe, ASIN B000AMSRU8

Elbow, Lippy Kids, Guy Garvey, Richard Jupp, Craig Potter, Mark Potter, Pete Turner, Build a Rocket Boys! CD, 2011, Polydor Ltd, ASIN B004H0N4PC

Manfred Mann, Do Wah Diddy Diddy, John Burgess, Manfred Mann, Manfred Mann Greatest Hits CD, 1996, UMTV, ASIN B0000071VP

www.cricketarchive.com

www.disused-stations.org.uk

www.richdickinsonsdf.co.uk

www.wikipedia.org